KETO BR

Easy and Delicious Low Carb and Gluten-Free Bakery Recipes for Every Meal to Lose Weight, Burn Fat and Transform Your Body

© **Jaida Ellison**

Legal & Disclaimer

TABLE OF CONTENTS

GLOSSARY OF BAKING TERMS

Bake: Cook with heat in an oven.

Batter: A mixture of flour, eggs, dairy, or other ingredients that is liquid enough to pour.

Beat: Stir together very rapidly to incorporate air. This can be achieved with a spoon, whisk, electric mixer, or food processor.

Blend: Stir ingredients together until well mixed.

Caramelize: Heat a sugar substance until it begins to turn brown.

Combine: Stir ingredients together until mixed.

Cream: Beat together sugar and butter until a light, creamy texture and color have been achieved. This method adds air to the batter, which helps the leavening process. Sometimes eggs are also added in the creaming step.

Cut In: Incorporating butter (or another solid fat) into flour until the fat transforms into small, granular pieces resembling coarse sand. This is achieved by using two knives in a cross-cutting motion, forks, or a special pastry cutter.

Drizzle: To pour a thin stream of a liquid on top of something.

Dust: Coat the surface of something by lightly sprinkling a dry substance (flour, sugar, cocoa powder, etc.).

Fold: Gently combine two substances in an effort not to deflate a delicate, lofty texture. Using a spatula, fold the bottom of the bowl up and over the top, turn the bowl 90 degrees, fold again, and repeat the process until combined.

Glaze: Coat with a thick, sugar-based sauce.

Grease: Coat the inside of a baking dish or pan with a fatty substance (oil, butter, lard) to prevent sticking.

Knead: Combine dough by hand on a hard surface. This involves folding the dough over, pressing it down, turning it 90 degrees and then repeating the process. Kneading mixes the dough and develops gluten strands that provide strength to loaves of bread and other baked goods.

Lukewarm: Slightly warm, or around 105°F.

Proof: Allowing bread dough to rise or yeast to activate.

Prove: To allow yeasted dough to rise.

Rolling Boil: Water that boils with large, fast, and vigorous bubbles.

Rub in: To integrate hard fat into flour by rubbing the two together with your fingertips until the mixture resembles breadcrumbs.

Scald: To pour over or immerse in boiling water for a short time in order to cook only the outer layer. Also, to bring milk almost to the boil, or to sterilise kitchen equipment with boiling water.

Score: Cut lines or slits into something.

Sift: To move a dry ingredient such as flour, sugar or cocoa through a sieve (sifter) to incorporate air and remove lumps or unevenly sized particles.

Slake: To mix a powder, such as cornflour, with a little liquid to form a paste in order for itto be mixed into a large amount of liquid without forming lumps.

Slurry – A term referring to a mixture of flour and water, which is stirred into soups and sauces as a thickener.

Softened: A solid, high-fat content substance that has been brought to room temperature in order to make it more pliable.

Soft Peaks: Egg whites or cream that has been whipped to the point that its peaks will bend or slump over to one side. To create a peak, pull the whisk or beater straight up and out of the foam.

Stiff Peaks: Egg whites or cream that has been whipped to the point at which a peak will stand completely erect. To create a peak, pull the whisk or beater straight up and out of the foam.

Temper: The process that takes chocolate through a temperature curve, which aligns the chocolate's crystals to make it smooth, silky and creates a satisfying snap when you bite into it.

Temper can also refer to the process where a small quantity of a hot liquid is incorporated into cold liquid to warm the cold liquid slightly.

Whip: Stir briskly with a whisk to incorporate air.

Whisk: A kitchen tool made of wire loops that tends to add air as it mixes substances together.

INTRODUCTION

General Overview

There is nothing more satisfying than the aroma of freshly baked bread coming out from the oven, wafting through the house. It is like saying welcome without a word being spoken. There is really no mystery to bread baking and it is probably one of the easiest things to do, even though most people may consider it a difficult task. Granted, it does take time, there is a saying, anything worth doing is worth doing well and is well worth the time.

If you can bake a loaf of bread, you can create your own recipe to satisfy your taste buds and preferences. There are just a few things to remember if you want to achieve the proper loaf. First of all, bread baking is nothing more than a chemical process that involves the use of wheat flour, yeast for rising, a sweetener to feed the yeast and warm water to provide a moist environment for the 'reaction' to occur. Therefore, there are only four basic ingredients that go into making a loaf of bread: flour, yeast, sugar and water. In addition, salt needs to be added for flavor and to keep the yeast from growing too rapidly.

The four basic ingredients plus salt are the only ingredients in your basic French bread. Other ingredients may be added to create different types of bread. For instance, if you add butter and eggs, you will have Challah or Egg Bread. Other ingredients that can be added include fruit, olives, onions, and molasses in place of sugar or honey.

There are numerous types of flours that may be used for baking bread. This includes all-purpose flour or bread flour, whole wheat flour and rye flour. Cornmeal can be substituted for flour and oats can also be used.

Yeast comes in dry granulated form and this is the easiest way to use it. It can also be purchased in cake form. The dry yeast is sold in the market in strips of 3 packages. Warehouse type stores also sell yeast in 1 lb. packages. If you are going to be doing a lot of baking, the one pound package is the way to go as it is much more economical. Store your yeast in the refrigerator and this will increase its shelf life.

Sweeteners that are commonly used in bread includes sugar, honey, molasses, and malt powder. You can also simply allow the yeast to derive its food from the sugar commonly found in the flour itself.

Liquid provides a growing medium for the yeast and acts as a binder for the other ingredients. The liquid is usually water but can also be milk. Fresh milk needs to be scalded before being used for bread making as the enzymes in the milk will inactivate the yeast and prevent the dough from rising to its full capacity. Evaporated or dried milk can also used instead as the enzymes are already deactivated.

Butter or oil are also used in some types of breads, it provides moisture, resulting in a longer shelf life.

Eggs enrich the dough and also help lighten it up. Bread made with eggs is not as heavy as the ones made without it.

You can start out by mixing the required amount of warm liquid with a sweetener and yeast in a large mixing bowl. Generally, a batch of dough that requires six cups of flour, 1 tbsp or a single package of yeast will be sufficient. Give the yeast about 5 - 10 minutes to proof. The yeast will start to grow and bubble. If the yeast shows no signs of life, discard it and buy a new pack.

Two to four ounces of butter or about 2 tablespoons of Olive Oil may be added to the proofed yeast. Then it is time to start adding the flour. The flour should be added in small increments and mixed in thoroughly before the next addition. You want to end up with soft dough that can be kneaded. If the dough is too stiff, you will not be able to knead it properly and it will be very heavy and not very digestible. Generally, 1 cup of liquid will be enough to absorb about 6 cups of flour.

One thing you should keep in mind when making bread is that not all flours are alike and that the weather can affect its absorption rate. When there is a lot of humidity in the air, more flour will be needed in comparison to a dry day.

Once a dough has formed (that is not sticky but is soft enough to knead) then it is time to put it on a floured surface and start kneading it. To knead the dough, you must use the heels of your hands (the firmest portion above the wrist). Start from the top and push with your heels and fold back with your fingers. Never knead with your fingers. First of all, there is not enough strength in your fingers to knead the dough properly and second of all, when you first start kneading the dough it will be soft and can ooze up between your fingers, making it a very difficult and messy job. As you are kneading, add flour as needed only to keep the dough from sticking. The kneading process will take about 10 minutes. When the dough is sufficiently kneaded, it will be soft and elastic. When you press on it, it will immediately return to its original position.

Once you are satisfied with the dough, place it in a large greased bowl and cover it up with plastic wrap or a clean dish towel. Place in a draft-free area and allow it to rise until it has doubled in bulk. This will take anywhere between 45 minutes to two hours, depending on the warmth of the air surrounding it. On warm days, the dough will rise very quickly and on cool days it will take longer.

Once the dough has risen, punch it down and knead it for about a minute. Allow it to rest for 5 minutes and then shape it into a loaf or two, if it is a large amount of dough. Generally speaking 6 cups of flour will make a very large loaf of bread or two smaller ones. The bread can be placed in greased loaf pans that have been sprinkled with cornmeal or can be free-formed on a flat baking sheet. Either way, make sure that the pans are greased or sprayed with a vegetable spray. The cornmeal will act as an interface, preventing the bread from sticking on the pan. It will also adds a textured interest to the bread.

Allow the shaped loaf to rise (covered with plastic wrap or a clean dish towel) in a warm place until doubled in bulk. Bake in a 375°F oven anywhere from 25-45 minutes depending on the ingredients and the size of the loaf. If you tap the baked loaf on the bottom it should sound hollow when it is done. You can also use an instant read thermometer to test the inside of the bread. It should reach 200°F. when it has finished baking. When the bread is done remove from the oven and allow to cool. When cool enough to handle turn the pan over (loaf pan) and place the bread on a cooling rack to finish cooling. If you bake the bread on a sheet pan, you can remove it with a large spatula.

When slicing hot bread, it is easiest to do it with a hot knife. Your knife blade can be heated by running it under a hot water faucet. However, you should allow your bread to cool for some time before slicing it as hot bread when sliced, may tend to be gummy. Cooling it down allows excess moisture to escape.

Hopefully these instructions will encourage you to try and make your own bread. There is no greater satisfaction than the aroma of freshly baked bread. And when you bite into a slice of fresh bread it is pure heaven!

What is Keto Bread?

Keto bread is just what it sounds like — it's bread, but it's not made from traditional wheat flour like regular bread is. Rather, keto bread is generally made using nut flours, which are high in protein and naturally low in carbs, so they won't disrupt your body's ketosis process.

Additionally, keto breads typically contain eggs for added protein and texture. But this also means that you have to be careful in the actual bread-making process to ensure that your ingredients are properly prepared and mixed, or otherwise your bread may end up with an "eggy" taste.

Just to give you an idea of the difference, one slice of basic keto bread made with almond flour is only one carb per serving —

whereas the average slice of white bread, something like what you'd buy at the store, has a whopping 35 carbs!

So when you're trying to stay under a certain number of carbs a day but, don't want to ditch breads, keto bread is one of the best ways to get that texture and taste without having to stress about your carb count.

TEXTURE TIPS FOR KETO BAKING

Ketogenic baking can be intimidating, especially if you have no baking skills or even if you are used to baking with wheat flour and sugar-based recipes.

Unfortunately, low carb baking is not as easy as swapping low carb ingredients for the high carb ones. Learning how to create keto baked goods can seem challenging at first but it's definitely a skill you want to acquire. So, it's worth the time and effort to learn.

1. Replace milk or water in recipes with buttermilk. Buttermilk will give a finer and overall lighter texture. Carbonated water also substitutes well for regular water in recipes such as pancakes - again giving it a lighter texture.

2. Unflavored gelatin can be used as a binding agent in baking - and it will help prevent crumbling. Remember to soften the gelatin in the liquid of the recipe before adding.

3. A combination of gluten free flours usually produces a better result than single flours.

4. To prevent crumbling you can use xanthan gum or guar gum in baking. Remember to add the gum to the dry ingredients. Note: some people have better results with the xathum gum as the guar gum can produce stomach ache in some.

5. Let your dough sit at least 30 minutes at room temperature to soften for a better texture in the final result.

In general there are a few basic differences in gluten-free baked goods that you will need to account for in converting old recipes. Gluten-free bread dough will be stickier and softer. If you try to make, it appear like your old recipe it will likely be too heavy, dry and crumbly. Also, the baking times will differ. Gluten free recipes tend to be better when baked for a longer period over a lower temperature. You may need to tent with foil to prevent overbrowning while allowing the entire bread or cake to cook through.

What Ingredients Do You Need To Make Keto Bread?

This keto bread is made with just 6 ingredients:

- Almond flour
- Coconut flour
- Melted butter
- Almond milk or Coconut milk from a carton, not the canned type
- Baking powder
- Salt (optional)
- Egg

The additional ingredients that you may add:

- Cheese (white cheddar, but mozzarella would wor too!)
- Finely chopped broccoli
- Spinach
- Feta cheese
- Bacon

THE BEST LOW CARB FLOURS AND SWEETENERS FOR ALL YOUR BAKING NEEDS

Flours

Almond Flour: Almond flour is one of the most common grain- and gluten-free flours. It's made from ground, blanched almonds, which means the skin has been removed. One cup of almond flour contains about 90 almonds and has a nutty flavor. It's commonly used in baked goods and can be a grain-free alternative to breadcrumbs. It can typically be substituted in a 1:1 ratio in place of regular or wheat flour. If you are baking with this type of flour, use one extra egg. Note that the batter will be thicker and your end product will be denser.

Almond flour contains many minerals, including iron, magnesium, calcium, potassium, copper, and manganese. It's also a good source of vitamin E and monounsaturated fat.

However, its fat content increases its calorie count to 640 per cup, which is 200 calories more than wheat flour.

Hazelnut Flour: Hazelnut flour is made by grinding hazelnuts. It can be a great substitute for almond flour. Some people prefer this low carb keto flour because it tends to be less grainy and produces a finer product. It is especially nice in cookie and cake recipes.

Sunflower Seed Flour: Sunflower seed flour is produced by grinding sunflower seeds finely, sunflower seeds can be a good low carb flour alternative if you are allergic to nuts. The taste of the sunflowers is pretty pronounced, so it may require using different brands to see which one you like best. Sunflower seed flour has a great quality in that it can be ground finely. And if you have a great blender, you could even make it at home.

However, it does have one negative pointer and it's that it tends to turn a shade of green when baked. This is because of a chemical reaction to baking powder or soda. This doesn't affect the flavor but it may not be as appealing to the eyes.

Sesame Seed Flour: Created by grinding sesame seeds finely, sesame seed flour is yet another great nut-free option. It is a little harder to come by and may require you make your own by grinding it yourself at home.

Coconut Flour: Coconut flour is a by-product of coconut milk actually when it's being produced. Once the coconut milk has been extracted, what's left is coconut meat. The coconut meat is then dried and finely ground. This creates a fine powder that looks a lot like wheat flour.

Sweeteners

Following a ketogenic diet in general involves cutting back on high-carb foods such as starches, desserts and processed snacks.This is essential to reaching a metabolic state called ketosis, which causes your body to start breaking down fat stores instead of carbs to produce energy. Ketosis also requires reducing sugar consumption, which can make it challenging to sweeten beverages, baked goods, sauces and dressings.

Fortunately, there are various low-carb sweeteners that you can enjoy.

Here are the 6 best sweeteners for a low-carb keto diet — plus 6 you should avoid.

Stevia: Stevia is a natural sweetener derived from the Stevia rebaudiana plant. It's considered a nonnutritive sweetener, which means that it contains little to no calories or carbs. Unlike regular sugar, animal and human studies have shown that stevia may help lower blood sugar levels. Stevia is available in both liquid and powdered forms and can be used to sweeten everything from drinks to desserts.

However, because it's much sweeter than regular sugar, recipes require less stevia to achieve the same flavor. For each cup (200 grams) of sugar, substitute only 1 teaspoon (4 grams) of powdered stevia.

Sucralose: Sucralose is an artificial sweetener that has not metabolized, meaning it passes through your body undigested and thus doesn't pack on calories or carbs.

Splenda is the most common sucralose-based sweetener in the market and it's quite popular because it lacks the bitter taste found in many other artificial sweeteners. While sucralose itself is calorie-free, Splenda contains maltodextrin and dextrose, two carbs that supply about 3 calories and 1 gram of carbs in each packet. Unlike other types of sweeteners, sucralose is not a suitable substitute for sugar in recipes that require baking.

Erythritol: Erythritol is a type of sugar alcohol — a class of naturally occurring compounds that stimulates the sweet taste receptors on your tongue to mimic the taste of sugar. It's up to 80% as sweet as regular sugar, yet it contains only 5% of the calories at just 0.2 calories per gram.

Additionally, though erythritol has 4 grams of carbs per teaspoon (4 grams), studies show that it may help lower blood sugar levels in your body. Moreover, due to its smaller molecular weight, it typically doesn't cause the digestive issues associated with other types of sugar alcohols.

Erythritol is used in both baking and cooking and can be substituted for sugar in a wide variety of recipes.Keep in mind that it tends to have a cooling mouthfeel and doesn't dissolve as well as sugar, which can leave foods with a slightly gritty texture.

Xylitol: Xylitol is another type of sugar alcohol commonly found in products like sugar-free gum, candies and mints. It's as sweet as sugar but contains just 3 calories per gram and 4 grams of carbs per teaspoon. Yet, unlike other sugar alcohols, the carbs in xylitol don't count as net carbs, as they don't raise blood sugar or insulin levels to the extent sugar does.

Xylitol can be easily added to tea, coffee, shakes or smoothies for a low-carb kick of flavor. It also works well in baked goods but may require a bit of extra liquid in the recipe, as it tends to absorb moisture and increase dryness. Because xylitol is as sweet as regular sugar, you can exchange it for sugar in a 1:1 ratio.

Note that xylitol has been associated with digestive problems when used in high doses, so scale back your intake if you notice any adverse effects.

Monk Fruit Sweetener: As its name implies, monk fruit sweetener is a natural sweetener extracted from the monk fruit, a plant native to Southern China. It contains natural sugars and compounds called mogrosides, which are antioxidants that account for much of the sweetness of the fruit. Depending on the concentration of mogrosides, monk fruit sweetener can be anywhere between 100–250 times sweeter than regular sugar. Monk fruit extract contains no calories and no carbs, making it a great option for a ketogenic diet.

Monk fruit sweetener can be used anywhere you would use regular sugar. The amount you use can vary between different brands based on what other ingredients may be included. While some recommend substituting using an equal amount of monk fruit sweetener for sugar, others advise cutting the amount of the sweetener in half.

Yacon Syrup: Yacon syrup comes from the roots of the yacon plant, a tuber widely grown in South America. The sweet syrup of the yacon plant is rich in fructooligosaccharides (FOS), a type of soluble fiber that your body is unable to digest. It also contains several simple sugars, including sucrose, fructose and glucose. Since your body doesn't digest a large portion of yacon syrup, it contains about one-third the calories of regular sugar, with just 20 calories per tablespoon (15 ml). Additionally, though it has about 11 grams of carbs per tablespoon (15 ml), studies show that the carbs in yacon syrup don't affect blood sugar the way regular sugar does.

Yacon syrup is best used as a sweetener in place of sugar in coffee, tea, cereal or salad dressings.

However, cooking with yacon syrup is not recommended, as the fructooligosaccharides can break down when exposed to high temperatures.

Sweeteners To Avoid On A Low-Carb Keto Diet

While there are plenty of options for low-carb sweeteners you can enjoy on a ketogenic diet, there are many others that aren't ideal.

Here are a few sweeteners that are high in carbs, can increase blood sugar levels and interrupt ketosis:

Maltodextrin: This highly processed sweetener is produced from starchy plants like rice, corn or wheat and contains the same amount of calories and carbs as regular sugar.

Honey: High-quality honey contains antioxidants and nutrients, making it a better choice than refined sugar. However, it's still high in calories and carbs and may not be suitable for a keto diet.

Coconut sugar: Made from the sap of the coconut palm, coconut sugar is absorbed more slowly than regular sugar. However, it's also high in fructose, which can contribute to impaired blood sugar control.

Maple syrup: Each serving of maple syrup packs a good amount of micronutrients like manganese and zinc, but it is also high in sugar and carbs.

Agave nectar: Agave nectar is about 85% fructose, which can decrease your body's sensitivity to insulin and contribute to metabolic syndrome, making it difficult for your body to regulate blood sugar levels.

Dates: This dried fruit is often used to sweeten desserts naturally. Despite supplying hefty amounts of fiber, vitamins and minerals, dates also contain a substantial amount of carbs.

THE TOOLS OF BREAD BAKING

The following are some of the basic tools you will need to get started baking bread. If you start to get into more advanced bread formulas and styles, additional tools may be needed, but for now these tools will set you off on the right track.

1. Scale

If you're a newbie baker then, I'm sure most bread recipes you've read have mentioned volume measurements i.e. 2 cups flour, 1 cup water, etc. There is a problem with measuring ingredients in this manner as the amount of an ingredient in one cup is almost never the same from cup to cup! In bread baking, especially when starting out, being precise is extremely important. Bread baking is hard enough to do consistently when all your ingredients are accurately measured. With volume measurements, you could be executing what is essentially a totally different recipe every time you make it! Why put yourself in a hole before you even get started?

This is where the scale comes in. With a scale, you will know exactly how much of an ingredient you're using every single time. This eliminates a lot of uncertainty right off the bat and puts you in a position to control your bread and not the other way around! Any competent professional baker uses a scale and there is no reason for you not to as well.

Another important benefit of measuring ingredients by weight is that you will be able to read bread formulas easily and understand if it is properly designed before doing anything. You can't do this with volume measurements. It just doesn't work. This is the key to being able to add any ingredient you want to your bread, be it an ancient grain, sunflower seeds, nuts, sugar, oil etc., and knowing it will work. You will be creating great bread and eliminating a significant amount of guess work.

2. Instant Read Thermometer

Just as we require precision while measuring our ingredients, we also need to be precise in regulating the temperature of our doughs. Temperature is a very important factor in bread baking. In fact, it is probably the most important factor behind scaling your ingredients accurately. The pace at which a dough moves from step to step through a recipe is completely dependent on what the dough temperature is.

Imagine you have a recipe that says "Let the dough rise for one hour." Well it could take an hour or it could take three hours! We don't know unless we know our dough is at the temperature the recipe calls for.

Temperature is even more important for a beginner baker who does not know how the dough has progressed to move on to the next step. All you have to rely on is the time stated in the recipe and if your temperature is off by even five degrees, then you might as well prepare a new batch. I saw the greatest improvement in my breads as a beginner when I started to get serious about temperature.

3. Mixing Bowls

You are going to need a place to mix your dough. You are also going to need a place to let it ferment. Mixing bowls are the perfect tool for both of these tasks. I would recommend plain metal bowls. No need to get anything fancy with rubber handles and all that. I like to have one extra large bowl to mix in. It gives a little more room to mix and keeps flour from flying all over the kitchen. Chances are you already have some mixing bowls around the kitchen.

4. Bowl Scraper / Dough Divider

This is possibly my favorite tool for bread baking. You can get by without a dough divider but once you have used it, you won't ever want to. Besides using it to divide dough, it is amazing for moving dough around the counter without leaving any behind or getting your hands all sticky. It makes dough handling infinitely easier. Eventually, it will become like an extension of your hand.

5. Loaf Pan

When starting out baking, I recommend starting with loaf bread baked in a loaf pan. Here are a few reasons that explain why:

Your shaping skills don't have to be as good to produce a great product. As a beginner, you should focus on getting the right feel of the dough as it moves through the stages of fermentation and how to handle it. Also, shaping bread using a loaf pan is much easier than shaping a free form loaf. If you make mistakes in shaping, the loaf pan will be much more forgiving.

It requires less oven set up. To bake a free form loaf at home you must have additional equipment such as a baking stone, a system to generate good steam in the oven and a method and tools for loading the loaf onto the stone. When you're a beginner it is a good idea to keep things simple. The loaf pan allows us to do this.

A single metal 9in x 5in or 4.5in x 8in loaf pan will work perfectly for baking loaf breads at home.

3 REASONS FOR CHOOSING KETO BREAD

Gluten is everywhere. It's in all the obvious places — like bread, pasta, and cupcakes — and it's the key to giving bread its chewiness and cupcakes their airy crumb. But this wheat protein can sneak into unexpected places like canned soup, salad dressings, and oatmeal. All ketogenic bread recipes are gluten-free so your health is not at risk.

Three major reasons why someone might need to give up gluten for health reasons include:

1. Celiac Disease

People with celiac disease have an immune reaction to the gluten in wheat, rye, and barley. This causes damage to the small intestine and interferes with the absorption of vital nutrients. Symptoms can be as mild as digestive problems and minor skin rashes or as severe as anemia, arthritis, and intense abdominal pain.

It's hard to pinpoint exactly how many people have celiac disease in the United States, mostly because so many people go undiagnosed, but most health experts put it in the range of 2 to 3 million people.

2. Gluten Intolerance

There are also a large number of people who have a sensitivity to gluten or are gluten intolerant. These people experience many of the same symptoms as those with celiac disease, but without the accompanying damage to the small intestine. There are also studies linking gluten intolerance to things like chronic fatigue, depression, irritability, and anxiety.

3. Wheat Allergy

A wheat allergy is a completely separate condition from gluten sensitivity or celiac disease. It's a histamine reaction to wheat, much like a peanut allergy or a shellfish allergy. People with this allergy usually present hives, rashes, or stomach pain after consuming wheat.

Why Is Keto Bread Recipe So Special ?

Most keto bread recipes lack a special ingredient that most high carb baked doughs have. It contains a special ingredient that will make your stomach growl on the first whiff.

Secret For The Best Keto Bread

The secret ingredient that makes a keto bread so good is actually the absence of yeast. This is what gives most keto bread recipes an edge over others.

The reason why yeast is not used in keto bread recipes is because it requires sugar to rise.

What most people don't know is that you can bake goods using a natural product called inulin instead.

Inulin (not "insulin") is a soluble prebiotic fiber that is food for the yeast to consume (like it feeds on sugar) allowing our keto bread recipe to rise and become soft and fluffy.

Why Add Yeast To Low Carb Bread Recipes?

There are three reasons we like to add yeast to some of our keto baked goods.

Keto Breads are typically dense and often grainy and dry. Yeast won't make it as light and fluffy as the high carb we're used to in the supermarket. But it does make it lighter and more doughy than other low carb bread.

Inulin that the yeast feeds on is a super prebiotic and has a multitude of health benefits.

The aroma - you can use yeast a number of times in your keto recipes purely for the aroma. The sense of smell is every bit as important as taste when it comes to the desirability of food.

KETOGENIC /GLUTEN FREE BREAD RECIPES

KETO BREAD MUFFINS

NOTE: ALL NUTRITIONAL VALUES ARE FOR ONE SERVING

1. Mediterranean Low Carb Egg Muffins With Ham

Prep Time: 10 Minutes

Cook Time: 15 Minutes

Total Time: 25 Minutes

Yield: 6 Muffins

These EASY Keto Low Carb Egg Muffins with ham have a Mediterranean flair and are packed with proteins! A portable, healthy and gluten free breakfast or snack!

30

Ingredients:

- 9 slices of thinly sliced deli ham
- 1/2 cup canned roasted red pepper, sliced + additional for garnishing
- 1/3 cup fresh spinach, minced
- 1/4 cup feta cheese, crumbled
- 5 large eggs
- Pinch of salt
- Pinch of pepper
- 1 1/2 tablespoon Pesto sauce
- Fresh basil for garnishing

Instructions:

- Preheat your oven to 400°F. Generously spray a muffin tin with cooking spray.
- Line each muffin tin with 1.5 pieces of ham, making sure you don't leave holes for the egg mixture to explode out of.
- Place a little bit of roasted red pepper in the bottom of each muffin tin.
- Place 1 tablespoon of minced spinach on top of each red pepper.
- Top the pepper and spinach off with a heaping 1/2 tablespoon of crumbled feta cheese.

- In a medium sized bowl, whisk together the eggs, salt and pepper. Divide the egg mixture evenly among the 6 muffin tins.
- Bake for 15-17 minutes until the eggs are puffy and feel set.
- Remove each cup from the muffin tin and garnish with 1/4 teaspoon of pesto sauce, additional roasted red pepper slices and fresh basil.

Recipe Notes

These aslo taste great cold if you want to eat them for breakfast or a quick snack.

Nutritional Values for 1 muffin:

Calories 188 Kcal

Total Fat 6.7g

Saturated Fat 2.4g

Protein 9.3g

Carbohydrates 1.8g

Dietary Fiber 1.8g

2. Cinnamon Walnut Flax Muffins

Prep Time: 10 Minutes

Cook Time: 20 Minutes

Total Time: 30 Minutes

Yield: 12 Muffins

Ingredients:

- 1 cup ground golden flax seed or buy flax meal already ground
- 4 pastured eggs
- 1/2 cup avocado oil or any oil
- 1/2 cup granulated sweetener (maple sugar erythritol, lakanto)
- 1/4 cup coconut flour
- 2 teaspoons vanilla extract
- 2 teaspoons cinnamon
- 1 teaspoon lemon juice
- 1/2 teaspoon baking soda
- Pinch of sea salt
- 1 cup walnuts chopped (okay to omit)

Instructions:

- Preheat over to 325°F.
- If starting with whole golden flax seed, grind it in a coffee grinder, then measure 1 cup.

Note: You can use golden flax seeds as the taste seems to be more mellow compared to dark brown flax seeds, but any color flax seed will work.

- Combine the ingredients together in a mixing bowl in the order they are listed. You can use an electric mixer if you'd like, but be sure to add in walnuts last, after using a mixer.

- Bake at 325°F for 18 to 22 minutes. I recommend using muffin liners to prevent sticking, plus they make the muffins more "portable".

Note: The data below is based on using a sugar alcohol to sweeten, if using coconut sugar, add 8 carbs and 30 calories per muffin.

Nutritional Values for 1 muffin:

Calories 219 Kcal
Total Fat 20g
Protein 6g
Carbohydrates 6g
Dietary Fiber 4g
Sugar 1g

3. Coffee Cake Muffins

Prep Time: 10 Minutes
Cook Time: 20 Minutes
Total Time: 30 Minutes
Yield: 12 Muffins

Coffee Cake Muffins are a delicious breakfast dessert or afternoon snack. These will tickle your taste buds any time of the day with cinnamon and butter crumbs.

Ingredients:

Batter:

- 2 tablespoons butter, softened
- 2 oz. cream cheese, softened
- 1/3 cup Trim Healthy Mama Gentle Sweet or my sweetener
- 4 eggs
- 2 teaspoon vanilla
- 1/2 cup unsweetened vanilla almond milk
- 1 cup almond flour
- 1/2 cup coconut flour
- 1 teaspoon baking powder
- 1/4 teaspoon salt

Topping:

- 1 cup almond flour
- 2 tablespoon coconut flour
- 1/4 cup Trim Healthy Mama Gentle Sweet or my sweetener
- 1/4 cup butter softened
- 1 teaspoon cinnamon
- 1/2 teaspoon molasses *** (optional)

Instructions:

- Preheat oven to 350°F. Line a standard muffin tin with paper liners and spray with cooking spray.
- In a food processor, combine all the batter ingredients. Mix thoroughly. Divide between the prepared muffin tin.
- Combine topping ingredients in the food processor and pulse until crumbs form. Sprinkle on top of the batter.
- Bake 20-25 min until golden. If the crumb topping starts to get too dark cover with foil for the last 5 minutes.

Recipe Notes

You can use of molasses for adding flavor, not sweetness. One teaspoon of molasses has 5 grams of carbs. This recipe uses 1/2 tsp divided by 12 servings. That is less than 25 grams of carbs from the molasses. If you want, you can omit it.

Notes on Sweeteners

You can use your own blend of xylitol, erythritol, and stevia in your recipes. This is twice as sweet as sugar. It is comparable to Trim Healthy Mama Gentle Sweet and Truvia.

Nutritional Values for 1 muffin:

Calories 222 Kcal
Total Fat 18g
Saturated Fat 6g
Protein 7g
Carbohydrates 9g

Dietary Fiber 4g

Sugar 1g

4. Low Carb Chocolate Zucchini Muffins

Prep Time: 10 Minutes

Cook Time: 30 Minutes

Total Time: 40 Minutes

Yield: 9 Muffins

Ingredients:

- 1/2 cup coconut flour
- 3/4 teaspoon baking soda
- 2 tablespoons cocoa powder
- 1/2 teaspoon salt
- 1 teaspoon cinnamon
- 1/2 teaspoon nutmeg
- 3 large eggs
- 2/3 cup swerve sweetener
- 2 teaspoons vanilla extract
- 1 tablespoon oil
- 1 medium zucchini, grated
- 1/4 cup heavy cream
- 1/3 cup Lily's chocolate baking chips

Instructions:

- Preheat the oven to 350°F.

- Line a 12 cup muffin tin with 9 cupcake liners and spray the inside of the liners with cooking spray.
- In a medium sized bowl, combine the coconut flour, baking soda, cocoa powder, salt, cinnamon, sweetener, and nutmeg.
- In a separate bowl, combine the eggs, vanilla, oil, cream, and zucchini.
- Add the wet ingredients into the dry ones and stir until combined. Fold in the chocolate chips.
- Spoon the batter into the muffin tins and bake for 30 minutes or until a toothpick comes out clean.
- Remove from oven and let it cool in the pan.

Nutritional Values for 1 muffin:

Calories 117 Kcal
Total Fat 7.7g
Carbohydrates 12.2g
Dietary Fiber 6.6g
Protein 3.9g

Recipe notes

These are very moist muffins so you will need to spray the inside of the muffin liners with cooking spray.

The zucchini is easy to grate with a box grater and you won't need to add any water.

5. Keto Pumpkin Spice Monkey Bread Muffins

Prep Time: 5 Minutes

Cook Time: 38 Minutes

Total Time: 43 Minutes

Yield: 10 Muffins

Ingredients:

For the dough:

- 2 cups shredded whole milk mozzarella cheese
- 2 tablespoons butter
- 3/4 cup superfine blanched almond flour
- 1/4 cup coconut flour
- 2 teaspoons baking powder
- 3 tablespoons granulated erythritol sweetener
- 1 teaspoon ground cinnamon
- 1/8 teaspoon ground nutmeg
- 1/4 teaspoon allspice
- 1/4 cup pumpkin puree
- 2 large eggs

To assemble:

- 1/2 cup swerve
- 2 teaspoons cinnamon
- Pinch of salt
- 2 tablespoons butter

- 2 tablespoons chopped pecans (optional)

Instruction:

For the dough:

- Preheat the oven to 350°F.
- Combine the almond flour, coconut flour, baking powder, sweetener, cinnamon, and nutmeg in a medium sized bowl and mix well.
- Combine the cheese and 2 tablespoons of butter in a large bowl. Microwave for 2 minutes. Stir well to combine.
- Add the dry ingredients to the melted cheese, along with the eggs and pumpkin purée.
- Stir well with a rubber spatula until a dough forms. Let the dough sit for 5 minutes.
- Meanwhile grease a muffin tin with butter.

To assemble:

- Combine the sweetener, cinnamon and a pinch of salt in a small bowl and mix well.
- Pinch off a small piece of dough and roll it into a ball about 3/4 inch in diameter.
- Roll the ball in the sweetener mixture and place it in a greased muffin cup.
- Repeat with two more balls for a total of three balls per muffin cup.

- Fill all ten cups with three coated dough balls each.
- Add the butter to the remaining sweetener and cinnamon mixture and microwave for 30 seconds.
- Stir and spoon a little of the butter mixture over each muffin.
- Top with chopped pecans if desired.
- Bake in the center of the oven for 30-35 minutes, or until golden brown and slightly firm to the touch.
- Remove and cool slightly before serving warm.

Recipe notes

Best served warm, these can be frozen and microwaved for 30 seconds when ready to eat!

Nutritional Values for 1 muffin:

Calories 187 Kcal

Total Fat 15g

Protein 9g

Carbohydrates 5g

Dietary Fiber 2g

6. Peanut Butter Chocolate Chip Muffins

Prep Time: 20 Minutes

Cook Time: 25 Minutes

Total Time: 45 Minutes

Yield: 6 Muffins

Ingredients:

- 1 cup almond flour
- 1/2 cup So Nourished erythritol sweetener
- 1 teaspoon baking powder
- 1 pinch salt
- 1/3 cup peanut butter
- 1/3 cup almond milk
- 2 large eggs
- 1/2 cup cacao nibs (or sugar-free chocolate chips)

Instructions:

- Preheat the oven to 350°F and combine all dry ingredients (except cacao nibs) in a large mixing bowl and stir.
- Add the peanut butter and almond milk and stir to combine.
- Add in 1 egg at a time, stirring until each is fully combined.
- Fold in the cacao nibs or sugar-free chocolate chips.
- Spray a muffin tin with cooking oil spray and even distribute the batter to make 6 large muffins.
- Bake for 20-30 minutes and let them cool completely. Enjoy with some butter or a drizzle of sugar-free maple syrup.

Nutrional Values for 1 muffin:

Calories 210 Kcal

Total Fat 13g

Protein 7g

Carbohydrates 3g

Dietary Fiber 2g

7. Low Carb Cinnamon Roll Muffins

Prep Time: 5 Minutes

Cook Time: 15 Minutes

Total Time: 20 Minutes

Yield: 20 Muffins

Ingredients:

- 1/2 cup almond flour
- 2 scoops vanilla protein powder, 32-34 grams per scoop
- 1 teaspoon baking powder
- 1 tablespoon cinnamon
- 1/2 cup nut or seed butter of choice almond butter, peanut butter, sunflower seed butter, etc.
- 1/2 cup pumpkin purée (can substituted for unsweetened applesauce, mashed banana or mashed cooked sweet potato)
- 1/2 cup coconut oil

For the glaze:

- 1/4 cup coconut butter

- 1/4 cup milk
- 1 tablespoon granulated sweetener
- 2 teaspoons lemon juice

Instructions:

- Preheat the oven to 350°F and line a 12-count muffin tin with muffin liners and set aside. This can also be made using a mini muffin tin.
- In a large mixing bowl, combine your dry ingredients and mix well. Add your wet ingredients and mix until fully incorporated.
- Evenly distribute the cinnamon roll muffin batter evenly amongst the muffin liners. Bake for 10-15 minutes, checking around the 10 minute mark by inserting a skewer in the center and seeing if it comes out clean. If it does, muffins are done. Allow it to cool in the pan for 5 minutes, before transferring to a wire rack to cool completely.
- Once cooled, prepare your cinnamon roll glaze by combining all the ingredients. Mix until thoroughly combined. Drizzle over the muffin tops and allow to firm up.

Recipe notes

Low Carb Cinnamon Roll Muffins should be kept refrigerated for optimum freshness. They can be kept at room temperature, in a covered container, but must be eaten within 2 days.

To freeze muffins, wrap each serving individually.

Nutritional Values for 1 muffin:

Calories 112 Kcal
Total Fat 9g
Protein 5g
Carbohydrates 3g
Dietary Fiber 1g

8. Double Chocolate Blender Muffins

Prep Time: 10 Minutes
Cook Time: 25 Minutes
Total Time: 35 Minutes
Yield: 9 Muffins

Ingredients:

- 3 large eggs
- 1/2 cup almond milk or water
- 1 teaspoon vanilla extract
- 1 cup almond flour
- 1/4 cup coconut flour
- 1/4 cup cocoa powder

- 1/4 cup Swerve Sweetener
- 2 teaspoons baking powder
- 1/4 teaspoon salt
- 1/4 cup avocado oil (or melted coconut oil)
- 1/3 cup sugar-free chocolate chips

Instructions:

- Preheat oven to 325°F and line 9 muffin cups with paper liners.
- In a blender, add the eggs, almond milk or water and vanilla extract. Blend briefly to combine.
- Add almond flour, coconut flour, cocoa powder, sweetener, baking powder and salt. Blend on medium high until smooth (you may need to scrape down sides of blender a little to make sure everything combines). Add melted coconut oil and blend until combined.
- Stir in all but 1 tablespoon of chocolate chips. Divide batter evenly among prepared muffin cups and top each with a few more chocolate chips.
- Bake 22 to 25 minutes, until firm to the touch. Remove and let it cool in pan.

Recipe Notes

This updated recipe uses liquid oil such as avocado oil, in place of the melted coconut oil. The coconut oil is delicious but it thickens the batter considerably, making it harder to get out of the blender.

Nutritional Values for 1 muffin:

Calories 92 Kcal

Total Fat 17.2g

Protein 5g

Carbohydrates 9.3g

Dietary Fiber 4.5g

9. Cheesy Garlic Bread Muffins

Prep Time: 20 Minutes

Cook Time: 25 Minutes

Total Time: 45 Minutes

Yield: 12 Muffins

Ingredients:

- 6 tablespoons butter, melted
- 5 cloves of garlic, pressed or finely minced, divided
- 1/2 cup sour cream
- 4 large eggs
- 1 teaspoon salt
- 3 cups almond flour
- 2 teaspoons baking powder
- 1 cup shredded Cheddar cheese, we used Cabot Seriously Sharp

- 1/4 cup chopped parsley
- 4 ounces shredded mozzarella
- Sea salt for sprinkling

Instructions:

- Preheat the oven to 325°F and grease a standard-size non-stick muffin tin well. Set the muffin tin on a large rimmed baking sheet (to catch the drips).
- Combine the melted butter and 3 cloves of the garlic. Set aside.
- In a high-powered blender or a food processor, combine the sour cream, eggs, remaining garlic, and salt. Process until well combined. Add the almond flour, baking powder, cheese, and parsley and process again until smooth.
- Divide half of the batter between the prepared muffin cups and use a spoon to make a small well in the center of each muffins.
- Divide the shredded mozzarella between the muffins, pressing into the wells. Drizzle with about 1 teaspoon of the garlic butter mixture.
- Divide the remaining batter between each muffin cup, make sure to cover the cheese as best as you can. Brush the tops with the remaining garlic butter and sprinkle with sea salt.

- Bake 25 minutes or so, until the tops are golden brown and firm to the touch. These will drip a lot of oil as they bake and it may spill over the sides a bit (hence the baking sheet underneath - to save your oven!).
- Remove and let it cool for 10 minutes before serving. They are fantastic when served still warm from the oven with the cheese still gooey. They are great cool too and warm up nicely.

Nutritional Values for 1 muffin:

Calories 332 kcal

Total Fat 27.2g

Saturated Fat 9.3g

Protein 12.8g

Carbohydrates 7.4g

Dietary Fiber 3.1g

10. Low Carb Blueberry English Muffin Bread Loaf

Prep Time: 15 Minutes

Cook Time: 45 Minutes

Total Time: 1 Hour

Servings: 12

Ingredients:

- 1/2 cup almond butter or cashew or peanut butter
- 1/4 cup butter ghee or coconut oil

- 1/2 cup almond flour
- 1/2 teaspoon salt
- 2 teaspoons baking powder
- 1/2 cup almond milk unsweetened
- 5 eggs beaten
- 1/2 cup blueberries

Instructions:

- Preheat oven to 350 °F.
- In a microwavable bowl, melt nut butter and butter together for 30 seconds, stir until combined well.
- In a large bowl, whisk almond flour, salt and baking powder together. Pour the nut butter mixture into the large bowl and stir to combine.
- Whisk the almond milk and eggs together then pour into the bowl and stir well.
- Drop in fresh blueberries or break apart frozen blueberries and gently stir into the batter.
- Line a loaf pan with parchment paper and lightly grease the parchment paper as well.
- Pour the batter into the loaf pan and bake 45 minutes or until a toothpick comes out clean from the center.
- Cool for about 30 minutes then remove from pan.
- Slice and toast each slice before serving.

Nutritional Values:

Calories 156 Kcal

Total Fat 13g

Saturated Fat 3g

Protein 5g

Carbohydrates 4g

Dietary Fiber 1g

Sugar 1g

11. Low Carb Gingerbread Blender Muffins

Prep Time: 20 Minutes

Cook Time: 25-30 Minutes

Total Time: 45-50 Minutes

Yield: 12 Muffins

Ingredients:

- 1/2 cup sour cream
- 4 large eggs
- 1 teaspoon vanilla extract
- 3 cups almond flour
- Sweetener equivalent to 3/4 cup sugar
- 1 tablespoon cocoa powder
- 2 teaspoons baking powder
- 2 teaspoons ground ginger
- 1 teaspoon ground cinnamon
- 1/4 teaspoon cloves
- 1/4 teaspoon salt

Instructions:

- Preheat the oven to 325°F and line a muffin tin with parchment or silicone liners.
- Combine the sour cream, eggs, and vanilla in a large blender jar. Blend about 30 seconds. Add the almond flour, sweetener, cocoa powder, baking powder, spices and salt. Blend again until well combined. If your batter is overly thick, add 1/4 cup water to thin it out.
- Divide the mixture among the prepared muffin cups and bake 25 to 30 minutes, until golden brown and firm to the touch.

Nutritional Values for 1 muffin:

Calories 205 kcal

Total Fat 17.1g

Protein 8.3g

Carbohydrates 6.7g

Dietary fiber 3.1g

KETO BREAD WITH GARLIC

NOTE: ALL NUTRITIONAL VALUES ARE PER SERVING

1. Keto Garlic Bread

Prep Time: 20 Minutes

Cook Time: 55 Minutes

Total Time: 1 Hour, 15 Minutes

Servings: 10

Ingredients:

Bread:

- 2/3 cup almond flour

- 2 1/2 tablespoons ground psyllium husk powder
- 1 teaspoon baking powder
- 1/2 teaspoon sea salt
- 1 teaspoon cider vinegar or white wine vinegar
- 1/2 cup boiling water
- 1 1/2 egg whites

Garlic butter:

- 2 oz. butter, at room temperature
- 1/2 garlic clove, minced
- 1 tablespoon fresh parsley, finely chopped
- 1/4 teaspoon salt

Instructions:

- Preheat the oven to 350°F. Mix the dry ingredients for the bread in a bowl.
- Bring the water to a boil, mixing the water, vinegar and egg whites to the bowl, while whisking with a hand mixer for about 30 seconds. Don't overmix the dough, the consistency should resemble Play-Doh.
- Form 10 pieces using damp hands and roll into hot dog buns. Make sure to leave enough space between them on the baking sheet to double in size.
- Bake on the lower rack in the oven for 40-50 minutes, they're done when you can hear a hollow sound when tapping the bottom of the bun.

- Make the garlic butter while the bread is baking. Mix all the ingredients together and put it in the fridge.
- Take the buns out of the oven when they're done and leave to let cool. Take the garlic butter out of the fridge. When the buns are cooled, cut them in halves, using a serrated knife, and spread garlic butter on each half.
- Turn your oven up to 425°F and bake the garlic bread for 10-15 minutes, until golden brown.

Nutritional Values:

Calories 93Kcal

Total Fat 9g

Protein 2g

Carbohydrates 3g

Dietary Fiber 2g

2. Cheesy Keto Garlic Bread

Prep Time: 10 Minutes

Cook Time: 15 Minutes

Total Time: 25 Minutes

 Servings: 10

Ingredients:

- 1 3/4 cup pre shredded/grated cheese mozzarella
- 3/4 cup almond meal/flour
- 2 tablespoons cream cheese full fat

- 1 tablespoon garlic crushed
- 1 tablespoon parsley fresh or dried
- 1 teaspoon baking powder
- Pinch salt to taste
- 1 egg medium sized

Instructions:

- Place all the ingredients apart from the egg, in a microwaveable bowl. Stir gently to mix together. Microwave on High for 1 minute.
- Stir then microwave on High for a further 30 seconds.
- Add the egg, then mix gently to make a cheesy dough.
- Place on a baking tray, ensuring it retains its shape. Cut slices into the low-carb garlic bread.
- Optional: Mix 2 tablespoons melted butter, 1 teaspoon parsley and 1 teaspoon garlic. Brush over the top of the low-carb garlic bread, sprinkle with more cheese.
- Bake at 425°F for 15 minutes, or until golden brown.

Nutritional Values:

Calories 117.4 Kcal

Total Fat 9.8g

Protein 6.2g

Carbohydrates 2.4g

Dietary Fiber 0.9g

Sugar 0.6g

3. Keto Garlic And Rosemary Focaccia

Prep Time: 15 Minutes

Cook Time: 22 Minutes

Total Time: 37 Minutes

Servings: 8

Ingredients:

- 2 oz. butter at room temperature
- 3 garlic cloves, finely chopped
- 1/2 teaspoon sea salt
- 1/2 teaspoon fresh rosemary, chopped
- 1 1/2 cups shredded mozzarella cheese
- 2 tablespoons cream cheese
- 1 teaspoon white wine vinegar
- 1 egg
- 3/4 cup almond flour
- 1/2 teaspoon salt
- 1/2 teaspoon garlic powder

Instructions:

- Preheat the oven to 400°F.
- Heat the mozzarella and cream cheese in a small pan on medium heat or in a microwave oven. Stir occasionally.
- Add the other ingredients and stir thoroughly.

- Flatten, the dough into a round crust, about 8 inches (20 cm) in diameter, on a parchment paper.
- Make holes in the dough with a fork and bake in the oven for about 12 minutes or until the bread has turned a golden color. Remove from the oven and let it cool a little.
- Mix together butter, garlic, salt, and rosemary. Spread on top of the bread and place in a round baking dish.
- Bake for another 10 minutes. Divide into 8–10 pieces and serve lukewarm.

Nutritional Values:

Calories 208 Kcal

Total Fat 19g

Protein 8g

Carbohydrates 2g

Dietary Fiber 0g

4. Keto Bread With Melted Garlic Butter

Prep Time: 20 Minutes

Cook time: 20 Minutes

Total Time: 40 Minutes

Servings: 8

Ingredients:

Bread:

- 3/4 cup coconut flour
- 2 tablespoons ground psyllium husk powder
- 1/2 teaspoon onion powder (optional)
- 1/2 teaspoon baking powder
- 1 teaspoon salt
- 1/3 cup melted coconut oil
- 2 cups boiling water
- Coconut oil, for frying (optional)
- Sea salt

Garlic butter:

- 4 oz. butter
- 2 garlic cloves, minced

Instructions:

- Mix all the dry ingredients in a bowl. Add oil and boiling water (hold some of it back in case it's too much) and stir thoroughly.
- Allow it to rise for five minutes. The dough will turn firm fairly quickly, but it will stay flexible. It should resemble the consistency of Play-Doh. If you find it too runny, add more psyllium husk until it looks right. If it's too firm, add some of the remaining water. The amount needed may vary depending on what brand of husk or coconut flour you're using.

- Divide it into 6 or 8 circular pieces, then use your hands to flatten it directly on parchment paper or on the kitchen counter.
- Fry rounds in a skillet over medium heat until the naan turns a nice golden color. Depending on your skillet you can add some coconut oil to it so the bread doesn't stick.
- Heat the oven to 140°F and keep the bread warm while you make more.
- Melt the butter and stir in the freshly squeezed garlic. Apply the melted butter on the bread pieces using a brush and sprinkle flaked salt on top.
- Pour the rest of the garlic butter in a bowl and dip pieces of bread in it.

Nutritional Values:

Calories 221 Kcal
Total Fat 22 g
Protein 2g
Carbohydrates 8g
Dietary Fiber 7g

KETO PIZZA BREAD RECIPES

NOTE: ALL NUTRITIONAL VALUES ARE PER SERVING

1. The Best Keto Pull Apart Pizza Bread Recipe

Prep Time: 10 Minutes

Cook Time: 25 Minutes

Total Time: 35 Minutes

Servings: 16

Ingredients:

- 2 1/2 cups mozzarella cheese shredded
- 3 eggs beaten
- 1 1/2 cup almond flour

- 1tablespoon baking powder
- 2 oz. cream cheese
- 1/2 cup grated Parmesan cheese
- 1 teaspoon rosemary seasoning
- 1/2 cup shredded mild cheddar or a cheese or your choice
- 1/2 cup mini pepperoni slices

Optional:

- Sliced jalapeños
- Non-stick cooking spray

Instructions:

- Combine the almond flour with the baking powder until it's fully combined.
- Melt the Mozzarella cheese and cream cheese. You can do this on the stove top or for 1 minute in the microwave.
- Once the cheese has melted, add the flour mixture and eggs and knead it until it forms into a sticky ball. I always use a silicone mat on the countertop to do this step.
- Once the dough has come together and all the ingredients are fully mixed, sprinkle the top of the dough with a small amount of parmesan cheese. This will help the dough not be so sticky when you start to handle it. I flip the dough over and sprinkle a small amount on the back side of the dough too.

- Form the dough into a ball and cut it in half. Continue cutting the dough until you get about 16 pieces from each side, a total of 32 pieces total (give or take).
- Roll the pieces of dough into equal sized balls then roll them in a plate of parmesan cheese that has been topped with a teaspoon of Rosemary seasoning. (This is the secret to forming the pull apart bread because the parmesan cheese coats each dough ball allowing it not to fully combine while it's baking. Plus, it adds an amazing flavor also.)
- Spray the bundt pan with non-stick cooking spray.
- Place the first layer of 16 prepared dough balls into a non-stick bundt pan.
- Then add a layer of your favorite shredded cheese, mini pepperoni slices, and jalapeño if desired.
- Add the next layer of 16 prepared dough balls on top of the first layer.
- Top the last layer with the rest of the shredded cheese, mini pepperoni slices, and jalapeños.
- Bake at 350°F for 25 minutes or until golden brown. It may take a bit longer if your bundt pan is thicker than the one I used.

Nutritional Values:

Calories 142 Kcal

Total Fat 9.4g

Protein 11.1g

Carbohydrates 3.5g

Dietary Fiber 1.5g

Sugar 0.8g

2. Microwave Pizza Bread

Prep Time: 10 Minutes

Cook Time: 2 Minutes

Total Time: 12 Minutes

Servings: 1

Ingredients:

- 1 tablespoon unsalted butter melted
- 1 large egg
- 1 tablespoon milk, can be substituted with almond milk
- 1 tablespoon superfine almond flour
- 1 tablespoon coconut flour do not substitute with almond flour
- 1/8 teaspoon baking powder
- 1/8 teaspoon Italian seasoning
- 1 tablespoon shredded parmesan cheese
- 1 tablespoon shredded mozzarella cheese
- 1 tablespoon low sugar tomato sauce optional
- 6-8 mini pepperoni

Instructions:

- In a large and wide (about 4 inches wide) microwave safe mug, add butter, egg, milk, almond flour, coconut flour, baking powder. Whisk until the batter is smooth. Stir in Italian seasoning and Parmesan cheese.
- Cook in the microwave at full power for about 90 seconds, or until the bread has cooked.
- Spread tomato sauce (if using) over surface of bread. Sprinkle mozzarella cheese over sauce. Place mini pepperoni on top of the cheese. Cook for an additional 30 seconds or until the cheese has melted. Enjoy while still warm.

Recipe Tips

Do not substitute coconut flour with almond flour. The recipe needs coconut flour to work. Coconut flour is highly absorbent and will absorb a lot of the liquid in the batter, which then helps form the bread.

Nutritional Values (1 pizza):

Calories 332 Kcal

Total Fat 25.5g

Saturated Fat 12.5g

Protein 16.1g

Carbohydrates 10.4g

Dietary Fiber 4.3g

Sugars 3.6g

3. 5 Minute Keto Pizza

Prep Time: 5 Minutes

Cook Time: 15 Minutes

Total Time: 20 Minutes

Servings: 1

Ingredients:

Pizza Crust:

- 2 large eggs
- 2 tablespoons parmesan cheese
- 1 tablespoon psyllium husk powder
- 1/2 teaspoon Italian seasoning
- Salt to taste
- 2 teaspoons frying oil (you can use bacon fat)

Toppings:

- 1 1/2 oz. Mozzarella Cheese
- 3 tablespoons Rao's Tomato Sauce
- 1 tablespoon Freshly Chopped Basil

Instructions:

- In a bowl or container, use an immersion blender to mix together all the pizza crust ingredients.

- Heat frying oil in a pan until hot, then spoon the mixture into the pan. Spread out into a cirlce.
- Once the edges have browned, flip and cook for 30-60 seconds on the other side. Turn the stove off, and turn the broiler on.
- Add tomato sauce and cheese, then broil for 1-2 minutes or until cheese is bubbling.

Nutritional Values:

Calories 459 Kcal

Total Fat 35g

Protein 27g

Carbohydrates 3.5g

Dietary Fiber 9g

4. Thin Crust Low Carb Pizza

Prep Time: 10 Minutes

Cook Time: 10 Minutes

Total Time: 20 Minutes

Servings: 1

Ingredients:

- 1 piece Low-Carb Pita Bread
- 2 tablespoons Rao's tomato Sauce
- 2 oz. low-moisture mozzarella cheese
- 1/8 teaspoon ground black pepper

- 1/8 teaspoon garlic powder
- 1/8 teaspoon chili flakes

Optional mix-in ideas: bacon, spinach, roasted red peppers, olives, artichokes, pesto, pepperoni, salami, prosciutto, roast beef, ham, avocado, sriracha, chili paste.

Instructions:

- Preheat oven to 450°F.
- Either brush slightly with oil or spray both sides with cooking spray.
- Place in oven for 1 to 2 minutes to harden and toast the crust.
- Remove from oven and add the sauce.
- Add cheeses (Mozzarella first).
- Add toppings of your choice.
- Rub with some olive oil and toast for 1-2 minutes at 450°F to crisp it.
- Cook for an additional 3-6 minutes to melt cheese.

Nutritional Values:

Calories 254 Kcal

Total Fat 16g

Protein 19.4g

Net carbs 7.8g

KETO BUN RECIPES

NOTE: ALL NUTRITIONAL VALUES ARE PER SERVING

1. Keto 3 MINUTE Burger bun

Prep Time: 1 Minutes

Cook Time: 2 Minutes

Total Time: 3 Minutes

Servings: 1 Bun

Ingredients:

- 3 tablespoons almond flour
- 1/2 teaspoon baking powder
- 1 1/2 tablespoon oil (I used olive oil)
- 1 egg

Instructions:

- In a small soup bowl, thoroughly mix the baking powder and almond flour ensuring that there are no clumps.
- Add the oil and egg.
- Beat it like you're making an omelet.
- Microwave on high for 90 seconds.
- At the end of 90 seconds, you will have a bun in the shape of the bottom of the bowl. Slice through the midsection with a bread knife so that you have a top.

Nutritional Values:

Calories 379 Kcal

Total Fat 35g

Saturated Fat 5g

Protein 9g

Carbohydrates 5g

Fiber 2g

2. Keto Hot Dog Bun

Prep Time: 10 Minutes

Cook Time: 50 Minutes

Total Time: 1 Hour

Servings: 10

Ingredients:

- 1 1/4 cup almond flour
- 5 tablespoons ground psyllium husk powder
- 2 teaspoons baking powder
- 1 teaspoon sea salt
- 2 teaspoons cider vinegar or white wine vinegar
- 1 1/4 cup boiling water
- 3 egg whites

Instructions:

- Preheat the oven to 350°F. Mix the dry ingredients in a bowl.

- Bring the water to a boil and add the water, vinegar and egg whites to the bowl, while whisking with a hand mixer for about 30 seconds. Don't overmix the dough, the consistency should resemble a Play-Doh.

- Form with moist hands into 10 pieces and roll into hot dog buns. Make sure to leave enough space between them on the baking sheet to double in size.

- Bake on lower rack in oven for 40-50 minutes, they're done when you hear a hollow sound when tapping the bottom of the bun.

- Serve with good quality hot dogs and toppings of your choice. Store the buns in the fridge or freezer.

Nutritional Values:

Calories 104 Kcal
Total Fat 8g
Protein 4g
Carbohydrates 4g
Dietary Fiber 3g

KETO COOKIES

NOTE: ALL NUTRITIONAL VALUES ARE PER SERVING

1. Keto Sugar Cookie Macaroons

Prep Time: 5 Minutes

Cook Time: 15 Minutes

Total Time: 20 Minutes

Servings: 12

Ingredients:

- 2 tablespoons butter, melted
- 1/4 teaspoon vanilla extract

- 8 drops Capella buttercream concentrate (omit if you want standard macaroons)
- 1 large egg
- 1/4 cup Swerve Confectioners
- 1/2 cup unsweetened macaroon coconut (or unsweetened shredded coconut)
- 2 tablespoons coconut flour
- Granular erythritol (to sprinkle on top; omit if you want standard macaroons)

Instructions:

- Preheat oven to 375°F.
- In a small bowl, combine melted butter, vanilla extract, buttercream extract (omit for regular macaroons), and an egg. Beat with a fork until everything is well combined. In a medium-sized bowl, combine Swerve Confectioners, macaroon coconut (or coconut flakes), and coconut flour. Mix until well combined.
- Add the wet ingredients to the dry and combine.
- Onto a non-stick cookie sheet or a cookie sheet covered with a non-stick silicone baking mat, scoop out tablespooon-sized macaroons. Then, sprinkle a bit of granular erythritol on top of each unbaked macaroon (omit for regular macaroons).
- Bake at 375°F for 12-15 minutes.
- Cool and enjoy!

Nutritional Values:

Calories 50 kcal

Total Fat 4g

Saturated Fat 3g

Protein 0g

Carbohydrates 1.7g

Dietary Fiber 1g

2. Low Carb Coconut Chip Cookies

Prep Time: 15 Minutes

Cook Time: 20-25 Minutes

Total Time: 35-40 Minutes

Servings: 16

Ingredients:

- 1 cup almond flour
- 1/2 cup cacao nibs
- 1/2 cup unsweetened coconut flakes
- 1/3 cup erythritol
- 1/2 cup almond butter
- 1/4 cup butter, melted
- 2 large eggs
- 20 drops liquid Stevia
- 1/4 teaspoon salt

Glaze (Optional):

- 1/4 cup heavy whipping cream
- 1/8 teaspoon guar gum
- 10 drops Liquid Stevia
- 1/2 teaspoon vanilla extract (optional)

Instructions:

- Pre-heat oven to 350°F. Mix together the dry ingredients: cacao nibs, almond flour, coconut flakes (unsweetened), erythritol and salt.
- Melt the butter in the microwave, then mix together all of the wet ingredients: butter, almond butter, eggs and liquid stevia. You can optionally add some vanilla extract during this step if you wish.
- Slowly pour the dry ingredients into the wet and mix together thoroughly.
- On a parchment paper lined baking sheet (or silpat), spoon out cookies evenly spaced. You should get about 16 cookies in total.
- Flatten the cookie dough with your fingers (or the back of a spoon). Don't over press the cookies, they should be about 1/3 inch thick.
- Bake cookies for 20-25 minutes or until the edges are golden brown. Remove from the oven and let it cool on a cooling rack.
- Optionally, create a glaze by combining the heavy cream, sweetener, and extract. Use a small mixer (or immersion

blender) to mix this together. Add the guar gum little by little while blending to thicken.

- Glaze the top of the cookies. The mixture should be relatively thick, but it's best to put in the refrigerator so that it solidifies more.
- Serve and enjoy!

Nutritional Values:

Calories 192 Kcal

Total Fat 17.4g

Protein 4.6g

Net carbs 2.2g

3. 3-Ingredient Peanut Butter Cookie

Prep Time: 10 Minutes

Cook Time: 10 Minutes

Total Time: 20 Minutes

Servings: 24

Ingredients:

- 1 cup peanut butter
- 1 teaspoon stevia powdered extract
- 1 egg

Instructions:

- Preheat oven to 350°F.

- Mix peanut butter, stevia, and egg together in a bowl using an electric mixer until smooth and creamy. Roll mixture into small balls and arrange on a baking sheet; flatten each with a fork, making a criss-cross pattern.
- Bake in the preheated oven for 10 minutes.
- Cool cookies on the baking sheet for 2 minutes before moving to a plate.

Nutritional Values:

Calories 96 Kcal

Total Fat 5.6g

Protein 3g

Carbohydrates 4.2g

Dietary Fiber 0.6g

4. Cheesy Herb Cookies

Prep Time: 10 Minutes

Cook time: 35 Minutes

Total Time: 45 Minutes

Yield: 8 Biscuits

Ingredients:

- 1 cup water
- 1 teaspoon granulated sugar substitute
- 1 tablespoon butter
- 1/2 cup shredded extra sharp cheddar

- 1/2 teaspoon salt
- 1/4 teaspoon black pepper
- 1/2 teaspoon dried oregano
- 1/4 teaspoon dried thyme
- 1/2 teaspoon garlic powder
- 1/4 teaspoon celery salt
- 3/4 cup coconut flour
- 1/4 cup almond flour
- 1/2 teaspoon baking powder
- 1/4 teaspoon xanthan gum
- 2 egg yolks
- 1/2 cup grated parmesan cheese

Instructions:

- In a small saucepan, bring the water to a boil along with the butter, sugar substitute, and cheddar cheese. Remove from the heat and set aside.
- Meanwhile, combine the salt, pepper, oregano, thyme, garlic powder, celery salt, coconut flour, almond flour, baking powder and xanthan gum in a small bowl and mix well.
- Add the dry ingredients to the liquid and stir until a dough forms.
- Add the egg yolks and stir until fully absorbed.
- Add the parmesan cheese and mix well – you may have to use your hands for this step.

- Divide the dough into 8 small (for traditional biscuit size) or 6 large (for hamburger bun size) balls and form into a biscuit shape (about 1 inch thick) with your hands.
- Place on a greased cookie sheet.
- Let the dough rest for at least 10 minutes.
- Bake in a preheated oven at 375°F for 25 minutes or until golden brown and puffed.
- Cool slightly before serving.

Nutritional Values:

Calories 197 Kcal

Total Fat 14g

Protein 11g

Net carbs 3.6g

5. Cheesy Keto Cookies

Cook Time: 20 Minutes

Prep Time: 20 Minutes

Total Time: 40 Minutes

Servings: 9

Ingredients:

- 2 cups almond flour
- 1 tablespoon baking powder
- 2 1/2 cups shredded cheddar cheese
- 4 eggs

- 1/4 cup half-and-half

Instructions:

- Preheat the oven to 350°F. Line a baking sheet with parchment paper.
- Combine almond flour and baking powder in a large bowl. Mix in Cheddar cheese by hand. Create a small well in the middle of the bowl; add eggs and half-and-half to the center. Use a large fork, spoon, or your hands to blend in the flour mixture until a sticky batter forms.
- Drop 9 portions of batter onto the prepared baking sheet.
- Bake in the preheated oven until golden, about 20 minutes.

Nutritional Values:

Calories 329 Kcal

Total Fat 27.1g

Protein 16.7g

Carbohydrates 7.2g

Dietary Fiber 0.6g

KETO BREAD BAGELS

NOTE: ALL NUTRITIONAL VALUES ARE PER SERVING

1. Low-Carb Cinnamon Sugar Bagels

Prep Time: 15 Minutes

Cook Time: 15 Minutes

Total Time: 30 Minutes

Yield: 6 Bagels

At only 5.6g net carbs per serving, these Low-Carb Cinnamon Sugar Bagels are about to be your new favorite breakfast! This recipe is low-carb, gluten-free, grain-free, vegetarian, and refined-sugar-free!

Ingredients:

- 1 3/4 cup almond flour
- 1/4 cup coconut flour
- 1 teaspoon baking soda
- 2 teaspoons cream of tartar
- 3 tablespoons golden monk fruit sweetener, divided
- 1 tablespoon cinnamon, divided
- 2 1/2 cups shredded mozzarella
- 2 oz. cream cheese
- 3 large eggs

Instructions:

- Preheat oven to 400°F and line baking sheet with parchment paper.
- In a large bowl, whisk together almond flour, coconut flour, baking soda, cream of tartar, 1 tablespoon golden monk fruit sweetener, and 1 teaspoon cinnamon.
- In a microwave-safe bowl, add mozzarella and cream cheese, and microwave for 90 seconds. Remove bowl

from microwave and stir ingredients together. Return to microwave and microwave for another 60 seconds. Stir together until mozzarella and cream cheese are completely combined.

- In a separate small bowl, whisk together 2 eggs. Add whisked eggs to the large mixing bowl of flour. Transfer cheese mixture to the large mixing bowl of flour and eggs. Using your hands, knead together the dough until well-combined (flour and cheese must be combined completely before moving ahead to remaining steps).

- Divide dough into 6 equal portions (you can use a food scale to make sure, mine were precisely divided). Using your hands, gently roll each of the 6 portions into a log shape, attaching the two ends to make the log into a circle. Place on a prepared baking sheet.

- In a bowl, whisk the remaining egg. Using a pastry brush, brush egg wash over bagels. Combine remaining 2 tablespoons of monk fruit sweetener and remaining 2 teaspoons cinnamon and sprinkle on top of the egg washed bagels (You used a mesh strainer to ensure cinnamon sugar is evenly coated on bagels).

- Bake bagels for 12-14 minutes, watching the bagels carefully the last few minutes to ensure the cinnamon doesn't burn. Remove bagels from the oven and allow it to cool for at least 15 minutes (NOTE: it is important to allow cooling time before eating as the inner part of the bagel will finish cooking during this time).

Nutritional Values:

Calories 307 Kcal

Total Fat 19.9g

Protein 25.4g

Carbohydrates 17.8g

Dietary Fiber 12.2g

2. Garlic Coconut Flour Bagels

Prep Time: 5 Minutes

Cook Time: 15 Minutes

Total Time: 20 Minutes

Yield: 6 bagels

Ingredients:

- 1/3 cup butter melted
- 1/2 cup coconut flour sifted
- 2 teaspoons guar gum or xanthan gum, optional
- 6 eggs
- 1/2 teaspoon garlic powder
- 1/2 teaspoon salt
- 1/2 teaspoon baking powder

Instructions:

- Blend together eggs, butter, salt, and garlic powder.

- Combine coconut flour with baking powder and guar or xanthan gum (if using).
- Whisk coconut flour mixture into batter until there are no lumps.
- Spoon into a greased donut pan.
- Bake at 400°F for 15 minutes.
- Cool on rack for 10-15 minutes then remove from pan.

Recipe notes

Bagel tastes better toasted.

Adding in a small amount of psyllium husks may give them less of a cake-like texture. And if psyllium is added, eggs can be reduced.

Nutritional Values:

Calories 191 Kcal
Total Fat 16g
Saturated Fat 9g
Protein 8g
Carbohydrates 6g
Dietary Fiber 3g

3. Keto Fathead Bagels

Prep Time: 20 Minutes
Cook Time: 20 Minutes
Total Time: 40 Minutes

These bagels are low carb, nut-free, and require only 5 ingredients to make. Easy and delicious, they will take your healthy breakfast to a whole new level.

Servings: 8

Ingredients:

- 1/2 cup coconut flour
- 2 teaspoons baking powder
- 3/4 teaspoon xanthan gum
- 12 oz. pre-shredded part skim mozzarella
- 2 large eggs

Optional Topping for Everything Bagels:

- 1 teaspoon sesame seeds
- 1 teaspoon poppyseed
- 1 teaspoon dried minced onion
- 1/2 teaspoon salt
- 1 tablespoon butter melted

Instructions:

- Preheat the oven to 350°F and line a large baking sheet with a silicone liner. In a medium sized bowl, whisk together the coconut flour, baking powder, and xanthan gum. Set aside.

- In a large microwave safe bowl, melt the cheese on high in 30 second increments until well melted and almost liquid. Stir in the flour mixture and the eggs and knead in the bowl using a rubber spatula.

- Turn out onto the prepared baking sheet and continue to knead together until cohesive. Cut the dough in half and cut each half into 4 equal portions so that you have 8 equal pieces of dough.

- Roll each portion out into a log about 8 inches long. Pinch the ends of the log together.

- In a shallow dish, stir together the sesame seeds, poppyseed, dried onion, and salt. Brush the top of each bagel with melted butter and dip firmly into the everything seasoning. Set back on the silicone mat.

- Bake for 15 to 20 minutes, until the bagels have risen and are golden brown.

Nutritional Values:

Calories 245 Kcal

Total Fat 21g

Protein 12g

Carbohydrates 6g

Dietary Fiber 3g

4. Keto Bacon Bagels

Prep Time: 10 Minutes

Cook Time: 18 Minutes

Total Time: 28 Minutes

Small bagels that are the perfect serving size for anybody that wants an easy breakfast that they can take with them out the door.

Servings: 3

This makes a total of 3 breakfast bagels. Each bagel is one serving.

Ingredients:

- 3/4 cup almond flour
- 1 teaspoon Xanthan gum
- 1 eggs
- 1 1/2 cup grated mozzarella cheese
- 2 tablespoons cream cheese
- 2 tablespoons pesto
- 1 cup arugula leaves
- 6 slices bacon
- 1 tablespoon salted butter
- 1 tablespoon sesame seeds

Instructions:

- Preheat oven to 390°F.

- In a bowl, mix together the almond flour and xanthan gum. Then add the egg and mix together until well combined. Set aside. It will look like a doughy ball.

- In a pot, over a medium-low heat slowly, melt the cream cheese and mozzarella together and remove from heat once melted. This can be done in the microwave as well.

- Add your melted cheese mix to the almond flour mix and knead until well combined. The Mozzarella mix will stick together in a bit of a ball but don't worry, persist with it. It will all eventually combine well. It's important to get the Xanthan gum incorporated into the cheese mix. If the dough gets too tough to work, place in the microwave for 10-20 seconds to warm and repeat until you have something that resembles a dough.

- Split your dough into 3 pieces and roll into round logs. If you have a donut pan place your logs into the pan. If not, make circles with each log and join together and place on a baking tray. Try to make sure you have nice little circles. The other way to do this is to make a ball and flatten slightly on the baking tray and cut a circle out of the middle if you have a small cookie cutter.

- Melt your butter and brush over the top of your bagels and sprinkle sesame seeds or your topping of choice. The butter should help the seeds stick. Garlic and onion powder or cheese make nice additions if you have them for savory bagels.

- Place bagels in the oven for about 18 minutes. Keep an eye on them. The tops should go golden brown.
- Take the bagels out of the oven and allow it to cool.
- If you like your bagels toasted, cut them in half lengthwise and place it back in the oven until slightly golden and toasty.
- Spread bagel with cream cheese, cover in pesto, add a few arugula leaves and top with your crispy bacon (or your filling of choice.)

Nutritional Values:

Calories 605.7 Kcal

Total Fat 50.3g

Protein 30.1g

Net Carbs 5.8g

KETO BREADSTICKS

NOTE: ALL NUTRITIONAL VALUES ARE PER SERVING

1. Keto Breadsticks

Prep Time: 20 Minutes

Cook Time: 13 Minutes

Total Time: 33 Minutes

Servings: 6

Ingredients:

Breadsticks dough:

- 1 1/2 cup part skim low moisture shredded mozzarella cheese
- 1 oz. cream cheese
- 1/2 cup almond flour
- 3 tablespoons coconut flour
- 1 large egg

Toppings:

- 1/2 cup part skim low moisture shredded mozzarella cheese
- 1/3 cup shredded parmesan cheese
- 1 teaspoon finely chopped parsley

Instructions:

- Preheat oven to 425°F.

- Add mozzarella and cream cheese to a large microwave-safe bowl. Melt in the microwave at full power in 30-second intervals. After every 30 seconds, stir cheese until it has completely melted and uniform (see photo above). This should take around 1-1 1/2 minutes total. Do not try to microwave the full time at once because some of the cheese will overcook. You can also melt the cheese over the stove in a double boiler.

- Add cheese ball to a food processor with dough blade attachment. Add in almond flour, coconut flour and egg. Pulse on high speed until the dough is uniform. The dough will be quite sticky, which is normal.

- Allow the dough to cool slightly, which will also make it less sticky and easier to work with. Roll the dough out between two sheets of parchment paper until 1/4 inch thick. Peel top sheet of parchment paper off of dough. Move the dough (still on the bottom parchment paper) onto a baking sheet.

- Spread 1/4 cup of mozzarella cheese over the dough, leaving a 1/2 inch perimeter. Bake for about 5-6 minutes, or until edges of the dough are golden and puffy.

- Evenly sprinkle the surface of dough with the remaining mozzarella cheese and parmesan cheese, leaving a 1/2 inch perimeter. Bake for 3-5 more minutes or until the cheese has is melted. Garnish with parsley before serving.

Recipe notes

I recommend using a food processor to make the dough because the dough is quite sticky so it's hard to mix by hand.

Because the dough is sticky, it's important to use parchment paper to roll out it as detailed in the instructions.

This recipe calls for both almond and coconut flour because the coconut flour helps absorb the liquid and the almond flour keeps the dough from being too sweet.

Nutritional Values:

Calories 207 Kcal
Total Fat 14.4g
Saturated Fat 5.9g
Protein 13.3g
Carbohydrates 7.4g
Dietary Fiber 2g
Sugars 2g

2. Low-Carb Braided Garlic Breadsticks

Prep Time: 20 Minutes
Cook Time: 12 Minutes
Total Time: 32 Minutes
Servings: 8

These Low-Carb Braided Garlic Breadsticks add garlicky goodness to any meal. This recipe works for low-carb, LC/HF, diabetic, Atkins, ketogenic, gluten-free, grain-free, and Banting diets.

Ingredients:

- 1 1/2 cup superfine almond flour
- 1/4 teaspoon xanthan gum
- 1 teaspoon grain-free baking powder
- 1/2 teaspoon garlic powder
- 1/2 teaspoon oregano
- 1/2 teaspoon salt
- 1 large egg
- 1 1/2 cup part-skim finely grated mozzarella cheese

Optional:

- Olive oil for brushing and additional sea salt to sprinkle on the top

Instructions:

- Preheat oven to 350°F. Line a cookie sheet with parchment. Have a rolling pin and two sheets of parchment about 18" long within reach.
- Prepare a double boiler. A medium saucepan with a medium bowl that will sit on top works fine for this purpose. Add about 2 inches of water to the saucepan or

lower part of the double boiler. Place over high heat and bring to a simmer uncovered. Once simmering, reduce heat to low.

- Meanwhile in the top-part of the double boiler (with it not over the water) combine the almond flour, xanthan gum, baking powder, garlic powder, oregano and salt using a whisk.

- Stir in the egg. The mixture will be very thick.

- Stir in the mozzarella cheese and place over the pot of simmering water. Be sure to protect your hands from the steam escaping to pot. I use a silicone mitten to hold the bowl.

- Stir the mixture constantly while the cheese melts and combines with the flour. As the cheese melts, it will combine with the almond flour mixture and will begin to look like bread dough.

- When the cheese has melted completely, transfer the dough to a prepared piece of parchment. Knead the dough a few times to completely combine the flour mixture and the cheese. Pat dough into a rectangular shape and cover with the second piece of parchment. Roll out dough into about a 14" X 18" rectangle. Remove top parchment.

- Slide the parchment containing the dough onto a cutting board. Using a serrated knife or a pizza cutter, trim off the most ragged edges. Cut the dough lengthwise in four equal pieces, then cut each of the four pieces into 3 strips. This should form 12 long strips. Cut these strips in half to form 24 shorter strips. Working with three strips at a time, fold the strips in half and pinch together, then pinch the ends of the three strips together at one end. Braid the three strips and pinch together at the other end.

- Repeat for the other strips.
- Transfer braids to the prepared baking sheet allowing at least half an inch between braids. Bake in preheated oven for 12-15 minutes or until edges are golden brown and the tops are lightly brown.
- Brush tops lightly with olive oil and sprinkle lightly with sea salt, if desired.
- Serve warm.

Nutritional Values:

Calories 192 Kcal

Protein 11g

Total Fat 16g

Carbohydrates 6g

Fiber 3g

3. 3 Ingredients Flourless Cheese Breadsticks

Prep Time: 15 Minutes

Cook Time: 25 Minutes

Total Time: 40 Minutes

Servings: 5

The easiest cheesy breadsticks you will ever make. You only need three ingredients to make these low-carb and gluten-free breadsticks.

Ingredients:

For the Breadsticks:

- 1 1/2 cup shredded mozzarella cheese
- 2 large eggs
- 1/2 teaspoon Italian seasoning

For the Topping:

- 1/2 cup shredded mozzarella cheese
- 2 tablespoons shredded parmesan cheese optional
- 1 teaspoon finely chopped parsley optional

Instructions:

- Preheat oven to 350°F. Line a 9 x 9 inch square baking pan with parchment paper.
- In a food processor, add 1 1/2 cups cheese, eggs and seasoning. Blend until everything is combined.
- Scoop out batter into baking pan. Carefully spread mixture until it evenly covers the bottom of the pan. Place into the oven and bake for about 20 minutes. The crust should be fairly firm with no wet dough remaining on top. Remove from oven and let it cool for a few minutes.

- Preheat oven to 425°F. Carefully remove crust off of parchment paper and place onto an oven-safe cooling rack. The cooling rack will help allow the bottom to crisp up. Sprinkle surface with remaining 1/2 cup cheese. If desired, you can substitute 2 tablespoons of mozzarella for 2 tablespoons of parmesan which gives it a little different flavor. Place cooling rack into the oven and cook breadsticks for about 5 minutes, or until cheese is melted and blistered.
- If desired, sprinkle with parsley before cutting and serving.

Recipe notes

You can add in other cheese blends for more variation but I recommend that the crust be mainly mozzarella cheese as some cheeses, like cheddar, can cause the crust to be too salty.

Nutritional Values:

Calories 142 Kcal

Total Fat 9.2g

Protein 11.4g

Carbohydrates 3.1g

Dietary Fiber 0.1g

Sugar 0.9g

KETO BREAD ROLLS

NOTE: ALL NUTRITIONAL VALUES ARE PER SERVING

1. Keto Hawaiian Sweet Bread Rolls Recipe

Prep Time: 10 Minutes

Cook Time: 20 Minutes

Total Time: 30 Minutes

Servings: 10

Ingredients:

- 1 1/2 cup almond flour
- 2 teaspoons baking powder
- 3/4 cup swerve powdered
- 3 cups mozzarella cheese shredded
- 3 oz. cream cheese
- 2 eggs
- 6 drops lorann pineapple oil
- 1 teaspoon fresh ginger paste

Instructions:

- Gather all of the ingredients first and measure them out. This is important because once you melt the mozzarella cheese you will need to combine the ingredients quickly before it cools down.

- Place the Almond flour, baking powder and Swerve into a medium size bowl and mix the ingredients until they are combined.
- Place the Mozzarella cheese and cream cheese in a microwave-safe container and cook it on high for about a minute and a half or until the cheese is melted. You can use a double broiler for this part if you prefer.
- Pour the melted cheeses mixture into the medium bowl filled with the dry ingredients.
- Add the eggs, fresh ginger paste, and Lorann Pineapple oil.
- Mix the ingredients until it's fully combined. The dough will be sticky.
- Place the dough on a silicone mat or parchment paper to continue kneading the dough together until forms. It will get less sticky as you knead it but it will always be a bit sticky.
- Cut the dough into 10 even parts.
- Roll each part into a ball.
- Place the dough ball into a well greased baking pan.
- Bake it at 425°F for about 15 to 20 minutes or until golden brown.
- Use a knife to separate the lines before you pull each roll out of the pan. The bottom of the rolls should have a nice brown crust.

Nutritional Values:

Calories 189 Kcal

Fat 12.3g

Protein 16.1g

Carbohydrates 6.2g

Fiber 2.4g

Sugar 1.6g

2. Oopsie Rolls

Oopsie rolls are a no-carb bread substitute. Their texture is spongy and their flavor is neutral, so they're very versatile.

Prep Time: 20 Minutes

Cook Time: 30 Minutes

Total Time: 50 Minutes

Yield: 6 oopsie rolls

Ingredients:

- Nonstick cooking spray
- 3 large eggs
- 1/4 teaspoon cream of tartar
- 3 oz. cream cheese, softened
- 1/4 teaspoon salt

Instructions:

- Preheat oven to 300°F. Line a cookie sheet with parchment paper and lightly spray it with nonstick spray.

- Separate the eggs, making sure no yolk gets into the whites and placing the whites in a clean, non-greasy bowl.
- Using a clean, non-greasy electric whisk, whip the egg whites and the cream of tartar until stiff.
- In a separate bowl, whisk together the yolks, cream cheese and salt, until smooth.
- Using a spatula, carefully fold the egg whites into the cream cheese mixture, working in batches. Work by placing a mound of egg whites on top of the yolk mixture, then gently fold the yolk mixture from under and over the egg whites, rotating the bowl, again and again until the mixture is incorporated. You want to use the folding technique because you want to keep the air bubbles intact in the egg whites.
- Spoon 6 large mounds of the mixture onto the prepared baking sheet. Gently press with a spatula on the top of each mound to flatten just slightly.
- Bake about 30 minutes, until golden-brown.
- Cool a couple of minutes on the cookie sheet, then gently transfer the oopsie rolls to a wire rack to cool completely. Oopsie rolls are best eaten on the day they are made. They do not store well.

Nutritional Values:

Calories 91.3 Kcal
Total Fat 8.1g

Saturated Fat 3.6g

Protein 4.2g

Carbohydrates 0.8g

Dietary Fiber 0g

Sugars 0.6g

3. The Best Keto Dinner Rolls

These are the best keto dinner rolls to help replace bread in your low carb lifestyle. This recipe is easy, filling, and delicious!

Prep Time: 5 Minutes

Cook Time: 10 Minutes

Total Time: 15 Minutes

Yield: 6 rolls

Ingredients:

- 1 cup mozzarella, shredded
- 1 oz. cream cheese
- 1 cup almond flour
- 1/4 cup ground flax seed
- 1 egg
- 1/2 teaspoon baking soda

Instructions:

- Preheat oven to 400°F.
- Line baking sheet with parchment, set aside.

- In a medium bowl, melt cream cheese and mozzarella together (microwave for 1 min).
- Stir cheeses together until smooth, add egg and stir until combined.
- In a separate bowl, combine the almond flour, ground flax seed and baking soda.
- Mix cheese and egg mixture into dry ingredients and stir until dough forms soft ball (it will be sticky).
- Using wet hands, gently roll dough into 6 balls.
- Roll tops in sesame seeds if desired and place onto a lined baking sheet.
- Bake for 10-12 minutes until golden brown.
- Let it cool for 15 minutes.

Recipe notes

Dough will be sticky but should be able to form balls. Use wet hands to roll balls. If it is too wet to mold then add an additional tablespoon of almond flour until pliable

4 large rolls work great for sandwiches and burgers, 6 smaller is good for dinner rolls

Rolls may seem soft coming out of oven but will firm up as they cool

Nutritional Values:

Calories 219 Kcal

Total Fat 18g

Protein 10.7g

Carbohydrates 5.6g

Dietary Fiber 3.3g

4. Vegan Keto Bread Rolls

 Prep Time: 15 Minutes

Cook Time: 1 Hour

Total Time: 1 Hour, 15 Minutes

Yield: 6 rolls

These Vegan Keto Bread Rolls are the most delicious, low-carb, and allergy-friendly way to enjoy bread! They can be topped with your favorite spread or cut in half and used as a bun! This recipe is keto, low-carb, paleo, dairy-free, egg-free, gluten-free, grain-free, vegetarian, vegan, refined-sugar-free, and has only 3.3g net carbs per roll!

Ingredients:

Flax Egg:

- 3 tablespoons ground flax seeds
- 1/2 cup + 1 tablespoon water

Bread Roll Dough:

- 1 1/4 cup almond flour
- 1/3 cup ground flax seeds
- 1/2 cup psyllium husk powder

- 1 teaspoon salt
- 2 1/2 teaspoons baking soda
- 1 1/4 teaspoon cream of tartar
- 1 1/4 cup water

Optional:

- 2 teaspoons sesame seeds

Instructions:

- Preheat oven to 375°F and line baking sheet with parchment paper.
- In a small bowl, add flax seeds and water and whisk together. Let it soak for 5 minutes.
- In a medium sized bowl, add dry ingredients and whisk together until fully incorporated. Add flax egg and mix with an electric mixer until well-combined.
- In a small pot, bring water to a boil.
- With the electric mixer turned on, slowly pour boiling water over dough mixture. Mix until all ingredients are combined. Let dough rest for 5 minutes.
- Form dough into 6 equal rolls.
- (Optional) To a shallow dish, add a small amount of water. To another shallow dish, add sesame seeds. Dip rolls one-by-one in water then sesame seeds to coat the top.
- Place rolls on a prepared baking dish and bakes for 50 minutes. Turn oven off and crack oven door. Allow rolls to

sit inside cooling oven for 10 additional minutes. Remove rolls from oven and allow to fully cool before serving.

Nutritional Values:

Calories 229 Kcal
Total Fat 14.6g
Protein 6.5g
Carbohydrates 23.6g
Dietary Fiber 20.3g

5. Keto Pull Apart Clover Rolls

Prep Time: 7 Minutes
Cook Time: 20 Minutes
Total Time: 27 Minutes

Keto Pull Apart Clover Rolls are the best low carb gluten free rolls that you can make. Soft, buttery, cheesy rolls that pull apart into three sections like a three leaf clover.

Servings: 8

Ingredients:

- 1 1/3 cup blanched almond flour or you can also use 1/3 cup coconut flour instead
- 1 1/2 teaspoonbaking powder
- 1 1/2 cup shredded Mozzarella cheese
- 2 ounces cream cheese

- 1/4 cup grated Parmesan cheese
- 2 eggs

Instructions:

- Grease or spray with non-stick oil spray a muffin pan and preheat oven to 350 °F.
- In a mixing bowl combine the almond flour and the baking powder, mix well. Set aside.
- Melt the shredded Mozzarella and the cream cheese on the stove top (or in the microwave for 1 minute) until melted.
- Once the cheese has melted, add flour mix, and eggs. Mix together.
- Grease hands and knead dough to form a sticky ball. Place the dough ball on a large sheet of baking paper or a silicon mat.
- Slice the dough ball into fourths. Then slice each quarter into 6 small pieces.
- Roll the small pieces into balls, and lightly roll the balls in a bowl of the Parmesan cheese to lightly coat them with Parmesan (this makes it easier to pull apart).
- Add 3 of the dough balls to each muffin cup in the muffin pan (this makes the 3 leaf clover).
- Bake at 350°F for 20 minutes.

Nutrional Values:

Calories 283 Kcal

Total Fat 21g

Saturated Fat 8g

Protein 16g

Carbohydrates 6g

Dietary Fiber 2g

Sugar 1g

OTHER KETO BREAD RECIPES

NOTE: ALL NUTRITIONAL VALUES ARE PER SERVING

1. Beer Bread

This bread is super easy, low in carbs and is a great addition to any meal. The beer flavor is present but definitely not over powering, so it pairs well with many different cuisines.

Prep Time: 10 Minutes
Cook Time: 45 Minutes
Total Time: 55 Minutes
Servings: 18, 1/2 inch slice

Ingredients:

- 2 cups ultra fine almond flour
- 1 tablespoon coconut flour
- 1 tablespoon Baking Powder
- 1/2 teaspoon salt
- 4 large eggs beaten
- 1/4 cup butter melted
- 1/2 cup beer

Instructions:

- Preheat your oven to 350°F and grease a 9x5 loaf pan with non stick spray.

- In a large bowl, combine the almond flour, coconut flour, baking powder, and salt.
- Add in the eggs, melted butter and beer. Stir until well combined.
- Pour the batter into the prepared pan, and bake for 40-50 minutes, or until a toothpick inserted into the center comes out clean.
- Allow to cool slightly before removing from the pan.

Nutritional Values for 1/2 inch slice:

Calories 105 Kcal

Total Fat 8.3g

Dietary Fiber 1.5g

Carbohydrates 3.2g

Protein 3.8g

2. Keto Blueberry Lemon Bread

Prep Time: 10 Minutes

Cook Time: 1 Hour, 5 Minutes

Additional Time: 15 Minutes

Total Time: 1 Hour, 30 Minutes

Servings: 12

Ingredients:

Keto Blueberry Lemon Bread Batter:

- 2 1/2 cups of finely milled almond flour

- 1 cup of sugar substitute
- 2 teaspoons of baking powder
- 1/2 teaspoon of sea salt
- 8 whole eggs
- 8 oz. of room temperature full-fat cream cheese
- 2 teaspoons of lemon extract
- 1/2 cup of room temperature unsalted butter
- 2 cups of fresh or frozen whole blueberries
- 1 tablespoon of lemon zest

Keto Lemon Glaze:

- 3/4 cup of confectioners sugar substitute
- 3 tablespoons of freshly squeezed lemon juice
- 2 tablespoons of heavy whipping cream
- 1 teaspoon of lemon extract
- 2 teaspoons of lemon zest

Instructions:

Keto Blueberry Lemon Bread:

- Preheat oven to 350°F.
- Grease and line with parchment paper a 10X5 inch loaf pan or two 6 inch loaf pans. (note if using two smaller pans check for doneness at 35 minute mark).

- In a medium-sized bowl, measure then sift the almond flour. To the sifted flour, add the baking powder, sea salt and stir. Set this aside.

- In a large bowl using an electric hand-held mixer or stand-up mixer blend the butter, cream cheese, and sugar-substitute until the mixture is light and fluffy.

- Next add the 8 eggs one at a time, making sure to scrape the bowl several times.

- To the wet batter, add the dry ingredients and combine until well-incorporated.

- Fold in the blueberries into the bread batter.

- Spread the batter into the greased loaf pan.

- Bake for 60-70 minutes or until an inserted toothpick comes out clean.

- Allow the loaf to cool in the pan for about 30 minutes before taking it out of the pan. Then let the pan cool on a baking rack for at least 60 minutes before adding the icing, refrigerating or freezing.

Keto Lemon Glaze:

- To make the lemon glaze, simply combine the confectioners sugar substitute, lemon juice, lemon extract, lemon zest and heavy whipping cream. Stir until fully incorporated.

Recipe notes

Baking times: For a 10X5 inch loaf pan 60-75 minutes. Check for doneness at the 60 minute mark and add foil and bake up to 15 minutes more if necessary.

For two 6 inch loaf pans, check for doneness at 35 minute mark and bake up to 45 minutes if necessary.

Nutritional Values:

Calories 350 Kcal
Total Fat 30.6g
Saturated Fat 11.4g
Protein 10.3g
Carbohydrates 7.2g
Dietary Fiber 3.5g
Sugar 2.3g

3. Nearly No Carb Keto Bread

A zero carb bread is almost impossible to make. But, this low carb pork rind bread comes pretty close to being zero carb.

Prep Time: 10 Minutes
Cook Time: 21 Minutes
Total Time: 31 Minutes
Servings: 12

Ingredients:

- 8 oz. cream cheese

- 2 cups mozzarella cheese grated
- 3 large eggs
- 1/4 cup parmesan cheese grated
- 1 cup crushed pork rinds
- 1 tablespoon baking powder

Optional:

- Herbs and spices to taste

Instructions:

- Preheat oven to 375°F. Line baking sheet (I used a 12 x 17 jelly roll pan) with parchment paper.
- Place cream cheese and mozzarella cheese in large microwaveable bowl.
- Microwave cheese on high power for one minute, stir, then microwave for another minute and stir again. The cheese should be fully melted.
- Add egg, parmesan, pork rinds, and baking powder. Stir until all ingredients have been incorporated.
- Spread mixture onto parchment paper lined pan. Bake at 375°F for 15-20 or until lightly brown on top.
- Allow pan to cool on rack for 15 minutes, then remove bread from pan and cool directly on rack.
- Slice into 12 equal sized pieces. Can be eaten plain or used to make sandwiches.

Nutritional Values:

Calories 166 Kcal

Total Fat 13g

Saturated Fat 7g

Protein 9g

Net carbs 1g

4. Flourless Peanut Butter Bread

Prep Time: 10 Minutes

Cook Time: 25 Minutes

Total Time: 35 Minutes

Servings: 12

This gluten-free bread flourless bread is easy to make with just five ingredients. It's a quick and easy bread option for those looking for something flourless, gluten free or low carb. It bakes, looks, feels and taste similar to wheat flour breads.

Ingredients:

- 1 cup smooth peanut butter
- 3 large eggs
- 1 tablespoon vinegar
- 1/2 teaspoon baking soda
- Sweetener equivalent to 1 teaspoon granulated white sugar

Instructions:

- Preheat oven to 350°F. Grease two 3 inch x 5-inch mini loaf pans. In a medium sized bowl, combine all the ingredients. Hand whisk or use a mixer to mix until everything is smooth.

- Divide batter equally between the two loaf pans. Bake for about 25 minutes until the breads are fully cooked or when a toothpick inserted comes out clean. Let breads cool before slicing and serving.

Nutritional Values:

Calories 148 Kcal

Total Fat 12.2g

Protein 6.3g

Carbohydrates 5.2g

Dietary Fiber 1.1g

5. Bakery Style White Bread

Prep Time: 10 Minutes

Cook Time: 45 Minutes

Total Time: 55 Minutes

Yield: 12

Ingredients:

- 1 stick of salted butter, softened
- 4 oz. cream cheese, softened

- 1 tablespoon Swerve granulated sweetener sugar substitute
- 3 large eggs
- 1/2 cup blanched almond flour
- 1 1/2 teaspoon baking powder
- 1/4 teaspoon salt

Instructions:

- Preheat oven to 350°F.
- Line a loaf pan with parchment paper & set aside.
- In a medium mixing bowl beat softened butter, cream cheese and Swerve sweetener. Add eggs one at a time, beating well after each addition.
- In small mixing bowl, combine almond flour, baking powder and salt and stir. Gradually add to cream cheese mixture, beating well.
- Spoon into parchment lined loaf pan. Bake for 45 minutes or until golden brown and set (ours took exactly 45 minutes).
- Allow to cool for 10 minutes and have a slice warm with butter. Heaven! Store wrapped in refrigerator.

Nutritional Values:

Calories 251 Kcal

Total Fat 4g

Protein 7g

Net carbs 3.1g

6. Low Carb Yeast Bread

This low carb yeast bread is soft and fluffy but it only has 5.4 net carbs per slice. Use it for sandwiches or toast, it's a great addition to your low carb lifestyle!

Prep Time: 20 Minutes
Cook Time: 40 Minutes
Total Time: 1 Hour
Servings: 12

Ingredients:

- 1 1/4 cups water 110°F - should feel comfortably warm
- Pinch of ground ginger
- 1 tablespoon yeast
- Sweetener equivalent to 1/2 teaspoon sugar
- 1 teaspoon of cider vinegar
- 2 tablespoons butter
- 3/4 teaspoon baking powder
- 1 teaspoon salt
- 1 cup vital wheat gluten
- 3/4 cup almond flour or pecan flour
- 1/4 cup coconut flour
- 1/4 cup flaxseed meal
- 1/2 cup dark rye flour

- 1/4 cup flax seed
- 1 teaspoon cardamom

Instructions:

- Mix 1/4 cup water, ginger, yeast, and sweetener. Set aside.
- Melt butter and set aside.
- Blend gluten, pecan or almond flour, coconut flour, flaxseed meal, and dark rye flour. Set aside.
- Yeast mixture should be bubbly.
- Add the yeast mixture and the remaining 1 cup of water to the bowl of a stand mixer fitted with the paddle attachment.
- On low speed add 1 1/2 cups of the flour mixture.
- Beat on low speed for 1 minute.
- Let stand for 10 minutes.
- Stir the salt, cardamom, and baking powder into the flour mixture.
- Stir the vinegar into the melted butter.
- With the mixer on low, add the butter mixture to the dough.
- Beat for 1 minute or until the liquid is mostly absorbed.
- Change to the dough hook.
- With the mixer on medium speed (or the kneading speed recommended by the manufacturer) slowly add the remaining flour mixture.
- The dough will begin to come together.

- Add the flaxseeds.
- Knead for 5 minutes (10 minutes if kneading by hand).
- When you are finished kneading the dough. "Pull back" when you gently pull some of it out.
- Grease a large bowl.
- Form the dough into a ball and grease it with butter.
- Place the dough into the bowl, cover with a towel and let it rise for 1 hour.
- Punch down, shape into a loaf and place in a greased loaf pan.
- Preheat the oven to 350°F.
- Let rise until the loaf is about 1 1/2-inches over the rim of the loaf pan, about 40 minutes.
- Bake for 40 minutes, or until an instant read thermometer stuck in the middle of the loaf registers 190°F.
- Let it cool in the pan for about 2 minutes, turn pan on it's side.
- Slide the loaf out and turn the loaf to the other side.
- Let it cool completely.
- Use a very sharp bread knife to cut into slices.

Nutritional Values:

Calories 165 Kcal

Total Fat 9g

Saturated Fat 2g

Protein 11g

Carbohydrates 9g

Dietary Fiber 4g

7. The Best Low Carb Keto Psyllium-Flax Bread

Prep Time: 15 Minutes

Cook Time: 1 Hour, 30 Minutes

Total Time: 1 Hour, 45 Minutes

Servings: 20

Ingredients:

- 10 oz. blanched almond flour
- 3 oz. Bob's Red Mill Golden Flax Meal
- 3/4 cup NOW Psyllium Husk Powder
- 1 tablespoon baking powder
- 1 teaspoon salt
- 8 oz. egg whites
- 3 oz. vinegar
- 14 oz. boiling water

Instructions:

Preparation:

- Preheat the oven to 350°F. Spray a 8x4 inch metal loaf pan with baking spray. Heat a kettle of water to a boil. Grind the golden flax meal in a coffee grinder to make sure it is very fine.

- Place a large bowl on a scale, turn it on, zero it out, and measure 10 oz. of almond flour into the bowl. Zero the scale and measure 3 ounces of golden flax meal into the bowl. Zero the scale and change it to grams. Measure 100 grams of psyllium powder into the bowl, then add the salt and baking powder. Remove the bowl from the scale and mix the ingredients with a hand mixer to ensure that they are evenly distributed.

- Put a smaller bowl in the scale, turn it on, zero it out and measure 8 oz. of egg whites into the bowl. Zero out the scale and add 3 oz. of vinegar.

- Pour the egg white mixture into the bowl with the dry ingredients and mix at a high speed until just combined. (The mixture will begin to expand a bit.) It should only take 10 seconds. DO NOT OVERMIX.

- Quickly rinse out the small bowl and return it to the scale. Zero the scale and add the 14 oz. of hot water. Pour the hot water onto the ingredients previously mixed with the egg whites (don't just dump it into the middle) and again, mix quickly at high speed, just until incorporated 10-15 seconds. If there is a little dry bread mix in the bottom of the bowl, it's okay.

Method: (Get ready. It's time to pay attention)

- Gently remove the dough with your hands, (it will be cool), ever-so-slightly and gently, shape it into a loaf shape while bringing it to the bread pan. Put the Psyllium-flax bread dough into the pan - it will not be perfect and there may be gaps in the corners or one side may be a little higher than the other - it's okay, put it into the oven.

- Bake for 80-90 minutes, depending on your oven. Depending on your oven, it may need a little more time. It is done when the internal temperature is 205-210°F.
- Let the loaf cool in the pan for only 5 minutes and then remove and place on a cooling rack to cool completely. If left in the pan to cool, the steam from the bread may make the loaf soggy. I place it on its side for 5 minutes, then set it right side up to finish cooling. Don't cut the bread until it is almost completely cool.
- Makes 20 slices with 3 net carbs per slice.

Storing:

- Store in an airtight bag in the refrigerator for about 10-12 days. The bread freezes beautifully. Thaw in the fridge. It's best to pan fry/toast the bread instead of using a toaster.

Recipe notes

People at high altitudes have had success cooking this bread in a toaster oven.

One commenter mentioned that removing the bread from the pan after cooking and putting it back in the oven for about 10 minutes helps dry out the bottom which has the tendency to compact a little and sometimes be more dense.

Nutritional Values:

Calories 127 Kcal

Total Fat 9g

Protein 5g

Carbohydrates 10g

Dietary Fiber 7g

8. Ursulas Delightful, Super low-carb bread

Prep Time: 5 Minutes

Cook time: 1 Hour

Total Time: 1 Hour, 5 Minutes

Servings: 10

Ingredients:

- 2 eggs
- 1/4 cup plain yogurt
- 2 cups ground almonds
- 1/2 cup sunflower seeds
- 1/2 cup sesame seeds
- 1 1/4 tablespoon oil
- Walnuts, chopped (add to your taste)
- 1/2 teaspoon salt
- 1 1/2 tablespoon chia seeds
- Bread seasoning, optional

Instructions:

- Preheat your oven to 340°F. Add your chia seeds to the yogurt and let them soak a bit, then mix in the egg yolks. Beat the egg whites until stiff, then fold in the yoghurt mixture. Now add all the remaining ingredients. Fill the mixture in a baking dish and bake at 340°F for about 1 hour.

Nutritional Values:

Calories 233 Kcal

Total Fat 20g

Protein 9g

Carbohydrate 8g

Dietary Fiber 4g

Sugar 1g

9. Keto Cinnamon Swirl Bread

This is the perfect low carb sweet bread! Enjoy it as a breakfast, snack or even dessert.

Prep Time: 15 Minutes

Cook Time: 30 Minutes

Total Time: 45 Minutes

Servings: 10

Ingredients:

- 4 eggs, separated

- 1/4 teaspoon cream of tarter
- 2 tablespoons butter, melted
- 2 tablespoons butter, softened
- 1 teaspoon vanilla
- 3 oz. cream cheese softened
- Liquid Stevia to taste, we used about 12 drops
- 1 teaspoon baking powder
- 1 cup almond flour
- 1 1/2 teaspoon cinnamon, divided
- 1/4 cup erythritol

Instructions:

- Preheat the oven to 350°F, and prepare a 9×5″ loaf pan with non stick spray.
- Separate the eggs into 2 large bowls.
- Add the cream of tarter to the egg whites and beat with an electric mixer until soft peaks appear. Set aside.
- Add softened butter, vanilla, cream cheese, and stevia to the egg yolks. Mix until well combined. Then add 1/2 teaspoon of cinnamon, baking powder and almond flour, stirring until well combined.
- In a small bowl, combine the melted butter, erythritol, and the remaining 1 teaspoon of cinnamon. Stir to combine and set aside.

- Fold the egg whites into the egg yolk mixture. This may take a few minutes as the egg yolk mixture may be fairly thick.

- Pour half of the egg mixture into the prepared loaf pan. Evenly top with the cinnamon and butter mixture, then the remaining egg mixture, ensuring that the mixture has been spread to the edges of the pan.

- Using a butter knife, make swirls into the bread, keeping the knife vertical to prevent too much mixing between the layers.

- Bake for 30-40 minutes or until the top is golden.

Nutritional Values:

Calories 161 Kcal

Total Fat 15g

Saturated Fat 6g

Protein 5g

Carbohydrates 3g

Dietary Fiber 1g

Sugar 1g

10. Chai Spiced Pumpkin Bread

Prep Time: 10 Minutes

Cook Time: 45 Minutes

Total Time: 55 Minutes

Chai Spiced Pumpkin Bread is a wondrous combination of pumpkin flavors and chai spices! No grains, gluten or sugar so it's low carb and keto friendly!

Servings: 12

Ingredients:

- 8 eggs
- 1 cup almond flour
- 3/4 cup coconut flour
- 1/2 teaspoon salt
- 2/3 cup + 1 tablespoon pumpkin puree
- 1 1/2 teaspoon baking powder
- 1/2 cup Lakanto Golden Monkfruit Sweetener
- 1 teaspoon baking soda
- 1 teaspoon vanilla extract
- 1 teaspoon cinnamon
- 1/2 teaspoon ground cardamom
- 1/4 teaspoon ground allspice
- 1/2 teaspoon ground ginger
- 1/4 teaspoon ground cloves
- 1/4 teaspoon black pepper
- 1/4 cup sour cream
- 5 tablespoons butter melted
- 1 tablespoon sunflower seeds optional
- 1 tablespoon sliced almonds optional

Instructions:

- Preheat oven to 350°F. Grease or spray a 8-9" loaf pan and line with parchment paper.

- Using a stand mixer and a whisk attachment, whip eggs until it's light, foamy, almost triple its original volume. This can also be done with a handheld mixer but use a large bowl to prevent splatter!

- If using a stand mixer, switch to paddle attachment. Add almond and coconut flours, salt, sweetener, baking powder, baking soda, pumpkin, and spices to the eggs and mix on medium speed until combined, scraping down the sides at least once. Add sour cream, melted butter, and extract to the batter and mix again till combined.

- Spoon the batter evenly into the prepared loaf pan and smooth out the top. If desired, sprinkle almonds and sunflower seeds evenly over the top of the batter. Bake at 350°F for 45 minutes to an hour or until a tester comes out clean. Half way through baking, cover it loosely with a foil to prevent over browning! If you use a 9" pan the baking time will be slightly shorter, so keep an eye on it starting at 30 minutes!

- Cool in the pan. Using the parchment, lift the loaf out of the pan and slice! Enjoy with a cup of coffee! This bread should be wrapped and stored in the fridge or it can be frozen whole or in slices.

Nutritional Values:

Calories 190 Kcal

Total Fat 14g

Saturated Fat 6g

Protein 7g

Total Carbohydrates 9g

Dietary Fiber 4g

Sugars 1g

11. Keto Pumpkin Bread

Prep Time: 10 Minutes

Cook Time: 50 Minutes

Total Time: 1 Hour

Servings: 10

A delicious, moist, keto pumpkin bread full of warm spices and amazing pumpkin flavor. Made with almond and coconut flours to keep it healthy, gluten-free, and low-carb.

Ingredients:

- 1/2 cup butter, softened
- 2/3 cup erythritol sweetener, like Swerve
- 4 eggs large
- 3/4 cup pumpkin puree, canned (see notes for fresh)
- 1 teaspoon vanilla extract

- 1 1/2 cup almond flour
- 1/2 cup coconut flour
- 4 teaspoon baking powder
- 1 teaspoon cinnamon
- 1/2 teaspoon nutmeg
- 1/4 teaspoon ginger
- 1/4 teaspoon cloves
- 1/2 teaspoon salt

Instructions:

- Preheat the oven to 350°F. Grease a 9"x5" loaf pan, and line with parchment paper.
- In a large mixing bowl, cream the butter and sweetener together until light and fluffy.
- Add the eggs, one at a time, and mix well to combine.
- Add the pumpkin puree and vanilla, and mix well to combine.
- In a separate bowl, stir together the almond flour, coconut flour, baking powder, cinnamon, nutmeg, ginger, cloves, salt. Break up any lumps of almond flour or coconut flour.
- Add the dry ingredients to the wet ingredients, and stir to combine. (Optionally, add up to 1/2 cup of mix-ins, like chopped nuts or chocolate chips.)
- Pour the batter into the prepared loaf pan. Bake for 45 to 55 minutes, or until a toothpick inserted into the center of the loaf comes out clean.

- If the bread is browning too quickly, you can cover the pan with a piece of aluminum foil.

Nutritional Values:

Calories 165 Kcal

Total Fat 14g

Saturated Fat 7g

Protein 5g

Carbohydrates 6g

Dietary Fiber 3g

Sugar 1g

12. Low Carb Keto Tortilla Recipe

Prep Time: 10 Minutes

Cook Time: 12 Minutes

Total Time: 22 Minutes

Servings: 6

Low Carb Keto Tortilla Recipe - Ultra low carb tortillas you can make yourself using cauliflower and cheese! These tasty tortillas are sturdy enough to hold all your ketogenic taco toppings!

Ingredients:

- 16 oz. raw cauliflower (about 1/2 a large head)
- 6 oz. shredded cheddar cheese
- 2 large eggs

- 1/2 teaspoon salt
- 1/4 teaspoon garlic powder
- 1/4 teaspoon onion powder

Instructions:

- Preheat the oven to 400°F. Line several baking sheets with parchment paper and set aside.
- Roughly chop the cauliflower and place it in the food processor. Pulse to grind the cauliflower into crumbs.
- Add all theremaining ingredients. Puree until all the ingredients come together into a smooth texture.
- Use a 3-tablespoon cookie scoop to portion the mixture onto the baking sheets, leaving plenty of room to roll them out.
- Cover the mounds with a piece of wax paper. Roll the mounds out into circles until they are about 4 to 4 ½ inches across. Remove the wax paper.
- Bake the tortillas for 12 minutes, until golden. Cool on the baking sheets for 3-5 minutes before peeling off the parchment paper.

Recipe notes

These tortillas are not great make-ahead meals. They taste best freshly baked within an hour of making.

Nutritional Values for 1 tortilla:

Calories 160 Kcal

Total Fat 11g

Saturated Fat 6g

Protein 10g

Carbohydrates 4g

Dietary Fiber 1g

Sugar 1g

13. Low-Carb Kalamata Olive Bread

Chewy, briny low-carb kalamata olive bread with all that Mediterranean flavor. It's perfect for making garlic breads, sandwiches, pizzas, or bruschetta. Best of all you can make it in just a few minutes in the microwave!

Prep Time: 2 Minutes

Cook Time: 2 Minutes

Total Time: 4 Minutes

Servings: 1

Ingredients:

- 1/4 cup egg whites beaten until frothy
- 1 tablespoon olive oil
- 1 1/2 tablespoon kalamata olive brine
- 2 tablespoons golden flaxseed meal
- 1 tablespoon almond meal
- 1/2 tablespoon coconut flour
- 1/2 tablespoon baking powder

- 1 pinch garlic powder
- 2 tablespoons chopped kalamata olives

Instructions:

- Beat the egg whites until frothy.
- Stir in the remaining ingredients.
- Pour into a greased coffee mug.
- Microwave on high for 1 to 2 minutes or until set but the top is moist.
- Allow it to cool for a few minutes before slicing.

Nutritional Values:

Calories 535 Kcal

Total Fat 45g

Protein 14g

Carbohydrates 9g

Dietary Fiber 5g

14. Multi-Purpose Low Carb Bread Recipe

Prep Time: 15 Minutes

Cook Time: 1 Hour, 15 Minutes

Total Time: 1 Hour, 30 Minutes

This might just be the best low carb bread recipe. You can use it for rolls, sticky buns and pizza!

Servings: 12

Ingredients:

- 1/2 cup coconut flour
- 1/2 cup almond flour
- 5 tablespoons psyllium husk powder (about 1.6 ounces)
- 1 tablespoon baking powder
- 1/2 teaspoon garlic or onion powder (optional)
- 1/2 teaspoon herbs like rosemary, oregano or basil. Pizza seasoning is great too! (optional)
- 1/4 teaspoon salt
- 1 1/2 cup egg whites (about 8 to 10 large egg whites)
- 3 tablespoons oil or melted butter
- 2 tablespoons apple cider vinegar
- 1/3 to 3/4 cup hot water

Instructions:

- Preheat oven to 350°F. If you are making a loaf, grease a 9x5 inch loaf pan well. If you are making rolls, line a large cookie sheet with parchment paper or a silicone liner.
- In a large bowl, whisk together the coconut flour, almond flour, psyllium husk powder, baking powder, and salt.
- Stir in egg whites, oil and apple cider vinegar. Slowly pour hot water over, stirring until dough expands. Start with the lesser amount and add a bit more until the dough

seems like it has expanded about 1.5 to 2 times. Do not add too much water or it can become a gloppy mess.

Loaf:

- For a loaf of bread, shape into a rough rectangle and place it in a prepared baking pan. Bake 60 to 75 minutes, until it has browned and the crust feels hard to touch (it will look done long before it really is. Don't take it out early or it will deflate). Remove and let it cool.

Rolls:

- Divide the dough into 10 to 12 equal pieces and roll it between your palms to create a rough ball. If dough is sticky, oil your palms with olive or avocado oil. Place on prepared cookie sheet. If you want flatter rolls for burgers or sandwich rolls, press it down to 1 inch thickness with your palm.
- Bake for 45 to 60 minutes, depending on the size and shape of the rolls. The rolls should be well browned and firm to touch. Remove and let it cool on the pan.

Nutritional Values:

Calories 97 Kcal

Total Fat 5.7g

Protein 4.1g

Carbohydrates 7.5g

Dietary Fiber 5.1g

15. Low Carb Gluten Free Cranberry Bread

A delicious gluten free low carb cranberry bread with fresh cranberries. This sugar-free bread uses a combination of stevia and erythritol sweeteners.

Prep Time: 10 Minutes

Cook Time: 1 Hour, 15 Minutes

Total Time: 1 Hour, 25 Minutes

Servings: 12

Ingredients:

- 2 cups almond flour
- 1/2 cup powdered erythritol or Swerve, see Note
- 1/2 teaspoon Steviva stevia powder, see Note
- 1 1/2 teaspoon baking powder
- 1/2 teaspoon baking soda
- 1 teaspoon salt
- 4 tablespoons unsalted butter melted (or coconut oil)
- 1 teaspoon blackstrap molasses optional (for brown sugar flavor)
- 4 large eggs at room temperature
- 1/2 cup coconut milk
- 1 bag cranberries, 12 oz.

Instructions:

- Preheat oven to 350°F; grease a 9-by-5 inch loaf pan and set aside.
- In a large bowl, whisk together flour, erythritol, stevia, baking powder, baking soda, and salt; set aside.
- In a medium sized bowl, combine butter, molasses, eggs, and coconut milk.
- Mix dry the mixture with the wet ingredients until well combined.
- Fold in cranberries. Pour batter into prepared pan.
- Bake until a toothpick inserted in the center of the loaf comes out clean, this might take about 1 hour and 15 minutes.
- Transfer pan to a wire rack; let the bread cool for 15 minutes before removing from pan.

Recipe notes

Sweeteners can be replaced with about 3/4 to 1 cup of any low carb sugar replacement depending on desired sweetness.

Nutritional Values:

Calories 179 Kcal
Total Fat 15g
Saturated Fat 4g
Protein 6.4g
Carbohydrates 7g
Dietary Fiber 2g

Sugar 1g

16. Caramel Frosted Banana Bread

Prep Time: 20 Minutes

Cook Time: 1 Hour, 15 Minutes

Total Time: 1 Hour, 35 Minutes

Servings: 16

Ingredients:

Banana Bread:

- 1/2 to 1 cup water
- 1/2 cup ground chia seed
- 2 cups almond flour
- 1/2 cup Swerve Sweetener
- 1/3 cup coconut flour
- 1/3 cup unflavoured whey protein powder
- 1 tablespoon baking powder
- 1/2 teaspoon salt
- 3/4 cup unsweetened almond milk
- 3 large eggs
- 1/4 cup melted butter
- 1 teaspoon banana extract (imitation would also be fine)
- 1/2 teaspoon vanilla extract
- 1/4 teaspoon stevia extract

Caramel Frosting:

- 4 oz. cream cheese softened
- 1/4 cup powdered Swerve Sweetener
- 6 tablespoons whipping cream
- 1 teaspoon caramel flavour OR vanilla extract

Instructions:

Banana Bread:

- Preheat oven to 325F and grease a loaf pan well.
- In a small bowl, combine 1/2 cup water and chia seed. Stir and let it sit to gel. If it remains very thick, add more water (it should resemble the consistency of mashed bananas).
- Meanwhile in a large bowl, whisk together almond flour, sweetener, coconut flour, whey protein powder, baking powder and salt.
- Stir in almond milk, eggs, melted butter, banana extract, vanilla, stevia and chia mixture until thoroughly combined.
- Spread mixture in prepared baking pan, smoothing the top.
- Bake 70 to 75 minutes or until golden brown until a tester inserted in the center comes out clean
- Let it cool in the pan for 20 minutes and then transfer to a wire rack to cool completely.

Caramel Frosting:

- In a large bowl, beat cream cheese and powdered sweetener until smooth.
- Beat in whipping cream and caramel or extract until well combined.
- Spread over cooled banana cake and let it set for about half an hour.

Nutritional Values:

Carbohydrates 9g
Dietary Fiber 5g

Unfrosted:

Calories 171 Kcal
Fat 13g
Protein 7g

Frosted:

Calories 215 Kcal
Fat 18g
Protein 8g

17. Keto Spinach Pesto Flat bread

Prep Time: 5 Minutes

Cook Time: 22 Minutes

Total Time: 27 Minutes

 Servings: 6

Ingredients:

- 1 cup of almond flour
- 2 1/2 cups of shredded mozzarella
- 2 oz. of cream cheese
- 2 tablespoons basil pesto
- 1 cup of chopped baby spinach
- Red pepper flakes, for topping

Instructions:

- Preheat oven to 350°F. Line large baking sheet with parchment paper and set aside.

- In a large bowl, mix almond flour, shredded mozzarella and cream cheese. Microwave for one minute or until melted.

- Using a spoon or rubber spatula, mix ingredients to form a ball. When the dough has cooled enough for you to handle, wet hands with a bit of water and pick up the dough ball. Knead it until smooth and all the ingredients have fully combined. (If your dough is too stiff or will not spread, it may be too cold. Place it back in the microwave for 5-10 seconds and it should be easier to spread).

- Use your hands to flatten the dough thinly across a parchment lined baking sheet. Bake the dough for 6 minutes or until it has slightly browned.

- Take the dough out of the oven and evenly spread it with pesto and spinach. Sprinkle red pepper flakes for a little kick!

- Return dough to oven and bake for an additional 16 minutes or until the edges are golden brown. Remove from the oven and sprinkle with shredded Parmesan before serving.

Nutritional Values:

Calories 295 Kcal
Total Fat 24.9g
Protein 16.4g

Carbohydrates 5.7g

Dietary Fiber 2.1g

18. Low Carb Corn Bread

Prep Time: 10 Minutes

Cook Time: 30 Minutes

Total Time: 40 Minutes

Servings: 8

Ingredients:

- 1/2 cup almond flour
- 1/4 cup coconut flour
- 1 teaspoon baking soda
- 3 eggs (large)
- 1/2 cup heavy whipping cream
- 1/4 cup salted cream butter (if you are using unsalted butter then make sure to add 1/2 teaspoon salt to your mixture)
- 1 teaspoon erythritol
- 1/2 teaspoon sweet corn extract

Optional Additions:

- Crumbled crispy bacon mixed into the batter
- Jalapeño slices on top of the batter
- Cheddar cheese 1/2 cup mixed into the batter

- Ground pepper mixed into the batter or sprinkled on top

Instructions:

- Preheat oven to 325°F.
- Mix all the ingredients together in a mixing bowl. If using optional toppings, add those as desired.
- Pour into a well seasoned 10-inch cast iron skillet. Bake for 30 minutes or until a toothpick comes out clean.
- Let it cool for 5 minutes and slice like a pie into 8 pieces and serve with butter.

Nutritional Values:

Calories 181 Kcal

Total Fat 16g

Saturated Fat 8g

Protein 4g

Carbohydrates 4g

Dietary Fiber 2g

19. Keto Almond Yeast Bread

Prep Time: 10 Minutes

Cook Time: 40 Minutes

Rising Time: 1 Hour

Servings: 16

Ingredients:

- 1 cup vital wheat gluten
- 1 1/4 cup almond flour
- 1 teaspoon salt
- 1 1/2 teaspoon baking powder
- 2 1/4 teaspoons dry yeast
- Sweetener equivalent 1/2 teaspoon sugar to activate the yeast
- 1 1/8 cup water luke warm 100°F
- 3 tablespoons oil

Instructions:

- In a mixing bowl, thoroughly mix all of the dry ingredients (gluten, almond flour, salt, baking powder dry yeast, & sugar).
- Add the water and oil, and mix into a dough.
- Knead for less than 3 minutes making sure that all of the ingredients are evenly combined. Note: if you knead the dough for too long it will get rubbery.
- Put the dough in an oiled bread pan and set in warm (100°F) oven for an hour to allow the dough to rise.
- Without punching the dough down, turn the oven up to 350°F and cook for 35 to 40 minutes.

Recipe notes

If you use a regular size bread pan (5"X3"X2") when the bread is done, it will have risen a little more than half of the pan height.

Double the recipe for a regular sized loaf.

A cocktail size bread pan (3-1/2"X 2-1/12"X 7-1/2") will rise above the top of the pan.

Nutritional Values:

Calories 107 Kcal

Total Fat 7g

Saturated Fat 1g

Protein 8g

Carbohydrates 3g

Dietary Fiber 1g

20. Easy Keto Sandwich Bread Recipe

Prep Time: 5 Minutes

Cook Time: 25 Minutes

Total Time: 30 Minutes

Servings: 12

Easy Keto Sandwich Bread Recipe - light, fluffy keto white bread perfect for slicing that toast beautifully. This is the perfect low carb bread!

Ingredients:

- 2 1/2 cups almond flour
- 2 cups whey protein
- 1 tablespoon xantham gum

- 3 teaspoons baking powder
- 1/2 teaspoon salt
- 1 1/4 cups warm water

Instructions:

- In a large mixing bowl, stir together the dry ingredients.
- Slowly add in the water and stir with a wooden spoon, stirring slowly as you add water, until the dough comes together.
- Pour the bread dough into a loaf pan that has been lined with parchment paper or greased well (be sure to double-check your cooking spray to ensure it is gluten free).
- Bake at 375°F for 20 to 25 minutes - until puffy and golden brown. You will see air bubbles on the sides of the bread, similar to how bread looks from inside.
- Remove from oven and let it cool completely on a rack before slicing.
- Only slice off the bread you're going to eat - pre-slicing bread will cause it to dry out or mold faster.
- Enjoy!

Nutritional Values:

Calories 197 Kcal

Total Fat 12g

Saturated Fat 1g

Protein 18g

Carbohydrates 8g

Dietary Fiber 3g

Sugar 2g

21. Almond Flour Bread

Prep Time: 5 Minutes

Cook Time: 45 Minutes

Total Time: 50 Minutes

Servings: 12

Ingredients:

- 2 egg whites at room temperature
- 2 eggs, white & yolk, at room temperature
- 2 cups almond flour
- 1/4 cup butter, melted
- 4 tablespoons psyllium husks or 2 tablespoons psyllium husk powder
- 1 1/2 teaspoon baking powder
- 1/2 teaspoon xanthan gum
- Pinch of salt
- 1/2 cup warm water

Instructions:

- Preheat your oven to 350°F.
- Beat the 2 eggs and the 2 additional egg whites. (You can reserve the 2 leftover yolks for mayonnaise).

- Add the rest of the ingredients and blend until you have a smooth dough. Don't over-mix.
- Fill into a lined baking tin (I used a small loaf pan 7 x 3.5 inch / 18 x 9 cm / 450 ml volume) and bake for 45 minutes or until a knife inserted comes out clean.

Recipe notes

You can use a regular 9 x 5 inch loaf pan for this almond flour bread recipe. It will come out a bit flatter than your regular toast slice though.

Low carb bread is filling and slices don't need to be the same size as regular wheat bread. That's why I purchased a small loaf pan for low carb baking. It's half the size of a regular loaf pan.

Check after 35 minutes - if the top of the bread starts browning too much, cover it with a piece of aluminium paper. This will prevent the top from getting too dark.

Nutritional Values:

Calories 160 Kcal
Total Fat 14.2g
Protein 5.7 g
Carbohydrates 4.1g
Dietary Fiber 3.5g

22. Keto coconut flour bread

Prep Time: 10 Minutes

Cook Time: 50 Minutes

Total Time: 1 Hour

Servings: 12

Ingredients:

- 8 tablespoons organic butter, melted
- 6 eggs
- 1/2 cup coconut flour
- 1 tablespoon erythritol
- 1 teaspoon baking powder
- 1/4 teaspoon salt

Instructions:

- Preheat oven to 350°F.
- Combine all of the dry ingredients (Coconut flour, Erythritol, Baking Powder & Salt). Crush any lumps in the flour with a fork.
- Whip the eggs with the whisk attachment in your standing mixer or by hand. Make sure the eggs have bubbles that can be popped. Don't over-mix to the frothy point or the batter will be too dry and will make your bread crumbly.
- Pour the melted butter into the egg mixture while you are still mixing on low.

- Carefully add the dry ingredients to the eggs while the mixer is on low.
- Pour or spoon batter into a prepared 8x4 inch bread pan.
- Bake at 350°F for 45-50 minutes or until golden brown.
- Let cool in the pan for 10-15 minutes before removing the bread.

Nutritional Values:

Calories 123 Kcal

Total Fat 10g

Saturated Fat 6g

Protein 3g

Carbohydrates 3g

Dietary Fiber 1g

23. 90 Second Keto Bread

Prep Time: 10 Minutes

Cook Time: 2 Minutes

Total Time: 12 Minutes

Servings: 2

Ingredients:

- 1/4 cup almond flour
- 1 tablespoon coconut flour
- 1 tablespoon melted butter or coconut oil for dairy free
- 1/8 teaspoon baking powder

- 1 large egg

Instructions:

- Place all the ingredients into a mug. Mix until combined with a fork.
- Microwave for 90 seconds, remove from the microwave, and loosen the bread from the edges of your mug using a knife.
- Flip the mug upside down, and cut into a total of 4 even slices.

Nutritional Values:

Calories 220 Kcal

Total Fat 21g

Saturated Fat 7g

Protein 4g

Carbohydrates 4g

Dietary Fiber 2g

24. Sesame Seed Keto Bread

Prep Time: 10 Minutes

Cook Time: 55 Minutes

Total Time: 55 Minutes

Servings: 8 (2 slices per serve)

Ingredients:

- 2 cups sesame seed flour (ground up sesame seeds work best)
- 7 large eggs
- 1/2 cup unsalted butter melted
- 1 teaspoon baking powder
- 1/2 teaspoon salt

Instructions:

- Preheat your oven to 355°F.
- In a large bowl, separate the egg yolks from the egg whites, beating the egg whites with an electric mixer until white and fluffy.
- In another bowl, mix together the melted butter, egg yolks, sesame seed flour, salt and baking powder.
- Gently fold the now complete egg yolk mixture into the egg whites, and gently mix together until it forms a uniform colour.
- In a bread loaf tin lined with baking paper, pour the mixture in and bake for 45 minutes, checking the center of the loaf with a skewer to ensure that its done.

To avoid cracking on the top of the loaf, place an ovenproof bowl of water in with the bread. This will ensure that the top of the bread loaf doesn't crack and stays in tact

Nutritional Values for 2 slices:

Calories 368 Kcal

Total Fat 30g

Protein 17 g

Carbohydrates 10g

Dietary Fiber 8g

25. Keto Seeded Bread

Prep Time: 10 Minutes

Cook Time: 40 Minutes

Total Time: 50 Minutes

Servings: 16

Ingredients:

- 7 large eggs
- 2 cups almond flour
- 1/2 cup unsalted butter
- 2 tablespoons olive oil
- 2 tablespoons chia seeds
- 3 tablespoons sesame seeds
- 1 teaspoon baking powder
- 1/2 teaspoon xanthan gum
- 1/4 teaspoon salt

Instructions:

- Preheat oven to 355°F.

- In a medium sized mixing bowl, whisk the large eggs together.
- Add the remaining ingredients, and mix together well. Using an electric hand whisk often helps with this recipe as the mixture can become quite thick.
- Pour into a loaf tin lined with baking paper. Place sesame seeds on top (optional).
- Bake for 40 minutes. (Remove once a skewer comes out of the middle clean).
- Can be sliced into 16 slices. Best kept in the fridge for up to 5 days, or frozen for up to 3 weeks.

Nutritional Values:

Calories 175 Kcal

Total Fat 16g

Saturated Fat 5g

Protein 6g

Carbohydrates 4g

Dietary Fiber 2g

Sugars 1g

26. Keto Chicken Fathead Bread

Prep Time: 5 Minutes

Cook Time: 25 Minutes

Total Time: 30 Minutes

Servings: 8

Ingredients:

For the dough:

- 1 1/2 cup mozzarella shredded
- 3/4 cup almond flour
- 1 tablespoon cream cheese

For the fillings:

- 1 tablespoon olive oil
- 1/2 medium onion chopped
- 1/2 cup heavy cream
- 1 1/2 cup chicken meat cooked, shredded
- 1/4 teaspoon ground coriander
- Salt and black pepper to taste
- 1 egg beaten
- 1 teaspoon sesame seeds

Instructions:

- Preheat oven to 425°F.
- Combine the almond flour, mozzarella, and cream cheese in a single bowl. Place in the microwave to melt for a minute, take out and mix with a spoon, and replace in the microwave for another minute.
- Saute the chopped onion in hot olive oil for about 2 minutes. Toss in the ground coriander and heavy cream together with the chicken meat. Season with pepper and

salt. Continue mixing for 2 minutes until the sauce thickens with no liquid left.

- Take out the mixture of almond flour and cheese and spread it in between 2 parchment papers. Flatten with a rolling pin. Remove the upper paper and spread the cooked chicken meat in the dough. Be careful with rolling the dough to avoid spilling the filling.

- Place the rolled dough in a heat-safe baking dish. Cover the dough with egg then top with plenty of sesame seeds. Take to the oven to bake and leave for 15 to 20 minutes until the bread becomes golden.

- Transfer to a serving plate and leave to cool for about 2 to 5 minutes. Cut into 8 slices and enjoy.

Nutritional Values:

Calories 250 Kcal
Total Fat 19g
Saturated Fat 7g
Protein 16g
Carbohydrates 3g
Dietary Fiber 1g

27. Keto Collagen Protein Bread

Prep Time: 10 Minutes
Cook Time: 30 Minutes
Total Time: 40 Minutes

Servings: 10

Ingredients:

- 1/2 cup Perfect Keto Collagen
- 5 egg whites and yolks separated
- 6 tablespoons coconut flour
- 3 tablespoons coconut milk full-fat
- 1 teaspoon xanthan gum
- 1 teaspoon baking powder keto friendly
- 1 pinch sea salt
- 1 tablespoon coconut oil melted (+ more for greasing)

Instructions:

- Preheat the oven to 325°F.
- In a bowl, combine all the dry ingredients.
- In a small bowl, whisk together coconut milk, egg yolks and melted coconut oil.
- In another bowl, whip egg whites until the peaks have formed.
- Fold both dry and wet ingredients in the whipped egg whites bowl and mix until incorporated.
- Brush your loaf dish (9x5x3-inch size) with coconut oil.
- Pour the batter into loaf dish and bake for 30 minutes.
- Let it cool completely and slice.

Nutritional Values:

Calories 98 Kcal

Total Fat 5g

Protein 7g

Carbohydrates 1g

Dietary Fiber 1g

28. Golden Keto Sesame Bread

Prep Time: 20 Minutes

Cook Time: 30 Minutes

Total Time: 50 Minutes

Servings: 8

Ingredients:

- 4 eggs
- 7 oz. cream cheese
- 2 tablespoons sesame oil
- 2 tablespoons light olive oil, and some more for brushing
- 1 cup almond flour
- 2 tablespoons ground psyllium husk powder
- 1 teaspoon salt
- 1 teaspoon baking powder
- 1 tablespoon sesame seeds
- Sea salt (optional)

Instructions:

- Preheat oven to 400°F.

- Beat cream cheese until fluffy. Add eggs, sesame oil and olive oil, mix until well combined.
- Add remaining ingredients except for the sesame seeds.
- Spread the dough in a baking tray (9" x 5" or 23 x 13 cm) greased with butter or lined with parchment paper. Let stand for 5 minutes.
- Brush with olive oil and sprinkle with sesame seeds and a touch of sea salt.
- Bake for about 30 minutes or until golden brown on top and not doughy in the middle.

Nutritional Values:

Calories 280 Kcal

Total Fat 26g

Protein 7g

Carbohydrates 4g

Dietary Fiber 2g

29. Low Carb Keto Jalapeno Cheese Bread

Prep Time: 2 Minutes

Cook Time: 15 Minutes

Total Time: 17 Minutes

Servings: 6

4 Ingredient Keto Jalapeno Cheese Bread is a simple, easy, and delicious low carb grain and flour free baked bread bursting with cheesy jalapeno flavor that tastes just like fresh baked bread

with only 1 carb per serving for an indulgent bread you can eat on a keto, paleo, or low carb diet!

Ingredients:

- 1 cup shredded cheese, cheddar, mozzarella, any kind of cheese that melts well
- 1/2 cup grated parmesan, or asiago, other hard, dry, grated cheese
- 2 eggs
- 1/4 cup jalapenos, rings, sliced, or diced

Instructions:

- Preheat oven to 375°F.
- Combine the shredded cheese and egg in a bowl and mix it until the ingredients are fully combined.
- Divide the mixture equally into four or six equal parts (depending on the size bread you want) on a baking sheet lined with parchment paper or a silicone baking mat.
- Bake at 375°F for about 15 to 20 minutes until the cheese has fully melted and created a slight brown crust.
- Feel free to mix up your cheese selection - but stick with one grated hard, dry cheese (like parmesan) to keep the flour-like texture.

Nutritional Values:

Calories 106 Kcal

Saturated Fat 4g

Protein 8g

Carbohydrates 1.5g

Dietary Fiber 1.7g

30. Cheesy Skillet Bread

Prep Time: 10 Minutes

Cook Time: 20 Minutes

Total Time: 30 Minutes

Servings: 10

Easy low carb skillet bread with a wonderful crust of cheddar cheese. This keto bread recipe is perfect with soups and stews.

Ingredients:

- 1 tablespoon butter for the skillet
- 2 cups almond flour
- 1/2 cup flax seed meal
- 2 teaspoons baking powder
- 1/2 teaspoon salt
- 1 1/2 cups shredded Cheddar cheese divided
- 3 large eggs lightly beaten
- 1/2 cup butter, melted
- 3/4 cup almond milk

Instructions:

- Preheat oven to 425°F. Add 1 tablespoon butter to a 10-inch oven-proof skillet and place in oven.
- In a large bowl, whisk together almond flour, flax seed meal, baking powder, salt and 1 cup of the shredded Cheddar cheese.
- Stir in the eggs, melted butter and almond milk until thoroughly combined.
- Remove hot skillet from oven (remember to put on your oven mitts), and swirl butter to coat sides.
- Pour batter into pan and smooth the top. Sprinkle with remaining 1/2 cup cheddar.
- Bake 16 to 20 minutes, or until browned around the edges and set through the middle. Cheese on top should be nicely browned.
- Remove and let cool 15 minutes.

Nutritional Values:

Calories 357 Kcal

Total Fat 31g

Protein 12.5g

Carbohydrates 7.2g

Dietary Fiber 4 g

31. The Best Cloud Bread Recipe

Prep Time: 10 Minutes

Cook Time: 20 Minutes

Total Time: 30 Minutes

Servings: 10

Cloud Bread is delicious, low carb, low fat, gluten free, and grain free... The Best Cloud Bread Recipe is a must-make this diet season!

Ingredients:

- 4 large eggs, separated
- 1/2 teaspoon cream of tartar
- 2 oz. low-fat cream cheese
- 1 teaspoon Italian herb seasoning
- 1/2 teaspoon sea salt
- 1/3 teaspoon garlic powder

Instructions:

- Preheat the oven to 300°F. If you have a convection oven, set on convect. Line two large baking sheets with parchment paper.
- Separate the egg whites and egg yolks. Place the whites in a stand mixer with a whip attachment. Add the cream of tartar and beat on high until the froth turns into firm meringue peaks. Move to a separate bowl.
- Place the cream cheese in the empty stand mixing bowl. Beat on high to soften. Then add the egg yolks one at a time to incorporate. Scrape the bowl and beat until the

mixture is completely smooth. Then beat in the Italian seasoning, salt, and garlic powder.

- Gently fold the firm meringue into the yolk mixture. Try to deflate the meringue as little as possible, so the mixture is still firm and foamy. Spoon 1/4 cup portions of the foam onto the baking sheets and spread into even 4-inch circles, 3/4 inch high. Make sure to leave space around each circle.

- Bake on convect for 15-18 minutes, or in a conventional oven for up to 30 minutes. The bread should be golden on the outside and firm. The center should not jiggle when shaken. Cool for several minutes on the baking sheets, then move and serve!

Recipe notes

The Best Cloud Bread Recipe can be stored in an airtight container in the refrigerator for several days. However the texture is best if eaten within 12 hours of baking.

Go easy on the garlic powder the first time you make it. I like adding 1/2 teaspoon, but that might be a little much for some palates.

Nutritional Values:

Calories 36 Kcal
Total Fat 2g
Saturated fat 1g

Protein 2g

Carbohydrates 0g

32. Savory Keto Bread Recipe

Prep Time: 5 Minutes

Cook Time: 35 Minutes

Total Time: 40 Minutes

Servings: 24

Ingredients:

- 2 1/2 cups almond flour
- 1/4 cup coconut flour
- 1/2 cup Kerrygold butter
- 8 oz. cream cheese
- 8 whole eggs set out at room temperature
- 1 teaspoon Rosemary seasoning
- 1 teaspoon Sage seasoning
- 2 tablespoons Parsley seasoning
- 1 1/2 teaspoon baking powder

Instructions:

- In a medium-size bowl, cream together the 1/2 cup of butter and 8 oz. of cream cheese until it has reached smooth consistency.

- Add 1 tsp. rosemary, 1 teaspoon sage, and 2 tablespoons parsley seasonings to the mixture and whip it until it has fully combined.
- Add the eggs and continue mixing the batter until it's smooth.
- Finally, add the flours, and the baking powder. The batter will be a bit thick.
- Grease 3 mini loaf pans. Fill each pan about 1/2 way with this savory batter. You can use the bigger loaf pans if you want but they will take longer to bake in the oven.
- Bake it at 350°F for about 35 minutes. (the large loaf pans take about 50-55 minutes) The bread should be golden brown on top and pass the toothpick test (stick a toothpick in the center of the dough and it should come out clean).

Nutritional Values:

Calories 202 Kcal
Total Fat 19.6g
Protein 5.6g
Carbohydrates 5.1g
Dietary Fiber 2.5g
Sugar 0.9g

33. Quick Low-Carb Bread

Prep Time: 10 Minutes

Cook Time: 10 Minutes

Total Time: 20 Minutes

Servings: 4

Ingredients:

- 1/4 cup crème fraîche
- 2 egg whites
- 2 teaspoons ground psyllium husk powder
- 1/2 cup almond flour
- 1/2 cup sesame seeds
- 1/4 cup sunflower seeds
- 1 1/2 teaspoon baking powder
- 2 pinches salt

Instructions:

- Preheat oven to 400°F.
- Mix egg whites and crème fraîche in a bowl.
- Add the remaining ingredients and work it into the egg batter. Let it rest for a few minutes.
- Form into piles and put in a baking dish. Sprinkle some extra sesame seeds if you like.
- Bake in oven for 10–12 minutes until golden brown.

Nutritional Values:

Calories 310 Kcal

Total Fat 27g

Protein 10g

Carbohydrates 9g

Dietary Fiber 4g

34. Keto Bread Twists

Prep Time: 10 Minutes

Cook Time: 20 Minutes

Total Time: 30 Minutes

Servings: 10

Ingredients:

- 1/2 cup almond flour
- 4 tablespoons coconut flour
- 1/2 teaspoon salt
- 1 teaspoon baking powder
- 1 1/2 cups shredded cheese, preferably mozzarella
- 2/3 oz. butter
- 1 egg
- 2 oz. green pesto
- 1 egg, for brushing the top of the bread twists

Instructions:

- Preheat the oven to 350°F.
- Mix all the dry ingredients in a bowl.

- Melt the butter and the cheese together on low heat. Stir with a wooden fork until the batter is smooth. Crack the egg and stir well.
- Add the dry ingredients and mix together into a firm dough.
- Place the dough between two sheets of parchment paper. Use a rolling pin and make a rectangle, about 1/5 inch thick.
- Remove the upper piece of parchment paper. Spread pesto on top and cut into 1-inch strips. Twist them and place on a baking sheet lined with parchment paper. Brush twists with the whisked egg.
- Bake in the oven for 15–20 minutes until they're golden brown.

Nutritional Values:

Calories 204 Kcal
Total Fat 18g
Protein 7g
Carbohydrates 3g
Dietary Fiber 2g

35. Keto French Toast

Prep Time: 5 Minutes
Cook Time: 3 Minutes
Total Time: 8 Minutes

Servings: 2

Ingredients:

Mug bread:

- 1 teaspoon butter
- 2 tablespoons almond flour
- 2 tablespoons coconut flour
- 1 1/2 teaspoon baking powder
- 1 pinch salt
- 2 eggs
- 2 tablespoons heavy whipping cream

Batter:

- 2 eggs
- 2 tablespoons heavy whipping cream
- 1/2 teaspoon ground cinnamon
- 1 pinch of salt
- 2 tablespoons butter

Instructions:

- Grease a large mug or glass dish with a flat bottom with butter.
- Mix all the dry ingredients together in the mug with a fork or spoon. Crack in the egg and stir in the cream. Combine until smooth and make sure there are no lumps.

- Microwave on high (approximately 700 watts) for 2 minutes. Check if the bread is done in the middle – if not, microwave for another 15-30 seconds.
- Let it cool and remove from the mug. Slice in half.
- In a bowl or deep plate, whisk together the eggs, cream and cinnamon with a pinch of salt. Pour over the bread slices and allow it to soak. Turn it around a few times so the bread slices absorb as much of the egg mixture as possible.
- Fry in plenty of butter and serve immediately.

Nutritional Values:

Calories 277 Kcal

Total Fat 23g

Saturated Fat 8g

Protein 15g

Net carbs 4g

36. Keto Cornbread

Prep Time: 10 Minutes

Cook Time: 20 Minutes

Total Time: 30 Minutes

Servings: 8

Ingredients:

- 1/4 cup coconut flour

- 1/3 cup oat fiber
- 1/3 cup whey protein isolate
- 1 1/2 teaspoon baking powder
- 1/4 teaspoon salt
- 4 oz. butter, melted
- 1/3 cup bacon fat or coconut oil, melted
- 1/4 cup water
- 4 eggs
- 1/4 teaspoon corn extract (optional)

Instructions:

- Preheat oven to 350°F. Place a greased 10-inch (25 cm) cast iron skillet in the oven to heat while you make the cornbread.
- Combine all the dry ingredients in a bowl.
- Add the melted butter, bacon fat, eggs, and water. Beat with a hand mixer. Stir in the corn extract.
- Pour the cornbread mixture into the hot cast iron skillet and bake for about 18 to 20 minutes or until lightly browned and firm to the touch.

Tips!

- The corn extract is optional, but provides a more authentic, corn-like flavor. If you don't have a cast iron skillet, a pie tin or small oven-proof skillet will work.

- Whey protein isolates has casein and lactose removed and is not the same as whey protein, which can be highly insulinogenic. Please check the ingredients on whey protein isolate to make sure there are no added sweeteners.
- Oat fiber is the pure insoluble fiber from the outer husk of the oat. Because it is not digestible, it does not impact blood glucose.

Nutritional Values:

Calories 240 Kcal

Fat 23g

Protein 7g

Carbohydrates 6g

Dietary Fiber 5g

37. Soft Keto Tortillas

Prep Time: 10 Minutes

Cook Time: 35 Minutes

Total Time: 45 Minutes

Servings: 6

Ingredients:

- 1 cup coconut flour
- 1/4 teaspoon baking soda
- 1/2 teaspoon salt
- 1/4 cup ground psyllium husk powder
- 1/2 cup avocado oil or olive oil
- 3 large egg whites
- 1 1/2 cup hot water

Instructions:

- Heat a large cast iron skillet or griddle medium heat.
- In a large bowl, sift together the coconut flour, baking soda and salt. Whisk in the psyllium husk.
- Drizzle in the oil slowly as you stir the mix, it will become moist and crumbly. Fold in the egg whites.
- Mix in the hot water half cup at a time, making sure it's thoroughly mixed in before adding more water. Combine until the dough looks and feels like moist play-doh.
- Shape 12 even-sized balls. Flatten the balls between parchment paper on a tortilla press or use a 6" pot and press them down.

- Cook 2 tortillas at a time on the large griddle by lying flat on the hot, dry cast iron and toasting 3 minutes a side, flipping once. Set aside until all the tortillas are done.

Nutritional Values:

Calories 250 Kcal

Fat 21g

Protein 6g

Carbohydrates 17g

Fiber 15g

38. Cranberry Feta Dough Balls

Prep Time: 15 Minutes

Cook Time: 35 Minutes

Total Time: 50 Minutes

Servings: 4

Ingredients:

- 1 cup mozzarella cheese grated
- 1/2 cup parmesan cheese grated
- 1/2 cup coconut flour
- 2 eggs beaten
- 1 cup Feta cheese crumbled
- 3 tablespoons cranberry chia jam
- 1/4 cup butter, melted unsalted

- 1/2 teaspoon baking powder
- 2 tablespoons chives, chopped optional garnish

Instructions:

- Preheat the oven to 400°F.
- In a bowl, mix the Mozzarella and Parmesan cheese together.
- Add the eggs and butter and mix thoroughly.
- Add the coconut flour and baking powder and mix until you almost have a dough like texture.
- Add the Feta cheese and cranberry chia jam, gently mixing this throughout the dough.
- Using your hands (clean!) make 15 even shaped balls for the tree shape. Anything left over can be used as the trunk if needed.
- Place the balls on a parchment covered baking tin in the shape of a Christmas Tree. You could try a festive wreath too!
- Bake for 30-35 until firm and golden.

Nutritional Values:

Calories 121 Kcal

Total Fat 9g

Protein 6g

Carbohydrates 3.7g

Dietary Fiber 1.9g

39. Cauliflower Low Carb Keto Grilled Cheese Sandwiches

Riced cauliflower can be used to make bread slices for low carb grilled cheese sandwiches. And, they are a cheesy comfort food that's simple to make.

Prep Time: 10 Minutes

Cook Time: 17 Minutes

Total Time: 27 Minutes

Servings: 4

Ingredients:

- One head riced cauliflower cooked
- 1 egg beaten
- 1 1/2 cup cheddar or Edam cheese grated
- 12 slices mozzarella Cheese
- 1/8 teaspoon dried sage
- 1/8 teaspoon dried oregano
- Dash of ground mustard seed
- Dash of dried thyme
- Ground black pepper
- Butter for greasing
- Fresh parsley for garnishing

Instructions:

- Strain excess liquid from cooked cauliflower rice.

- Combine riced cauliflower, beaten egg and 1/2 cup of the grated cheese in a bowl then sprinkle some pepper, mustard seed, sage, oregano and thyme. Mix well.

- In a slightly greased baking sheet, form cauliflower mixture resembling a slice of bread. This recipe made 4 slices, about 1/2 inch thick for each slice. More slices for thinner pieces.

- Bake cauliflower slices in a preheated oven of 350°F for about 10 to 12 minutes.

- In a skillet, melt butter at low heat and lay one slice of cauliflower "bread," cover with slices of mozzarella cheese, sprinkle with the grated cheese, then top with slices of mozzarella cheese and cover with another slice of cauliflower "bread."

- Cover skillet and watch closely as the mozzarella cheese melts over low heat. Occasionally check the bottom side to avoid burning. If the heat may seem too low, turn to medium heat but move the queso de bola cauliflower "bread" at the sides then cover the skillet again.

- Flip to the other side and continue to melt mozzarella cheese. Edam cheese doesn't melt quickly so it will just blend with the melted mozzarella cheese. Use multi-serving wide flat/wide-slotted tongs to safely flip the cauliflower sandwich.

- Once the mozzarella has melted to your desired consistency, transfer it on a plate, garnish with parsley and enjoy!

Nutritional Values:

Calories 503 Kcal

Total Fat 37g

Saturated Fat 22g

Protein 33g

Carbohydrates 9g

Dietary Fiber 2g

40. Gluten-free, Low Carb and Keto Grilled Cheese Waffles

Prep Time: 15 Minutes

Cook Time: 20 Minutes

Total Time: 35 Minutes

Servings: 8

Extra light and crisp, these gluten free and keto grilled cheese waffles are easy and quick to make .

Ingredients:

- 1/2 cup almond flour
- 4 1/2 tablespoons golden flaxseed meal finely ground (or coconut flour)
- 1 1/2 tablespoons whey protein isolate or psyllium husk
- 3/4 teaspoon xanthan gum
- 1/2 cup water
- 3 tablespoons grass-fed butter or coconut oil

- 1/2 teaspoon kosher salt
- 3 eggs lightly beaten
- 1 1/2 teaspoon baking powder
- 1 3/4 teaspoon paprika optional
- 1/3 teaspoon garlic powder to taste, optional
- 1/4 teaspoon onion powder optional
- 6 oz. cheddar cheese grated, to taste

Instructions:

- Whisk together in a medium sized bowl the almond flour, finely ground flaxseed meal, whey protein and xanthan gum. Set aside.

- Heat up water, butter and salt in medium pot (or Dutch oven) until it just begins to simmer. Turn the heat to low and add in the flour mixture, mixing constantly to incorporate. Continue to cook and stir until the dough pulls away from the pan and forms into a ball, 1-3 minutes.

- Transfer dough back to the bowl and allow it to cool for 5 minutes. The dough should still be warm, but not hot enough to scramble the eggs.

- Add in one egg at a time, mixing with an electric mixer until fully incorporated. Mix in baking powder and spices (optional, but highly suggested!). Mix in 1/2 of the grated cheese, the dough should be very elastic.

- Heat up and butter your waffle iron well. Spoon in a thin layer of the batter, sprinkling remaining cheese, and topping off with another thin layer of batter. It will be thick, so spread it out using a wet spatula (or wet the back of a spoon). Close waffle iron and cook for 8-12 minutes on high until fully golden and cooked through.
- The waffles are best freshly made, but they can be stored in an airtight container in the fridge for a couple days. And the dough can be kept in the fridge for a day or two.

Nutritional Values:

Calories 188 Kcal

Total Fat 16g

Saturated Fat 7g

Protein 8g

Carbohydrates 2g

Dietary Fiber 1g

41. Keto Baguette Recipe

This recipe is as close as you are going to get without kicking your body out of ketosis.

Prep Time: 10 Minutes

Cook Time: 45 Minutes

Total Time: 55 Minutes

Servings: 3

Ingredients:

- 1/3 cup almond flour
- 1/4 cup psyllium husk powder
- 1/3 cup coconut flour
- 1/2 teaspoon baking soda
- 1 teaspoon salt
- 1 teaspoon xanthan gum

Dry ingredients:

- 3 egg whites
- 1 whole egg
- 1/4 cup low-fat butter-milk
- 2 tablespoons Apple Cider Vinegar
- 1/3 cup lukewarm water

Instructions:

- Preheat the oven to 360°F. Mix all of the dry ingredients together into a bowl.
- In a different bowl, mix the buttermilk, egg whites and eggs together with an electric beater.
- Add the egg mixture to the dry ingredients and mix well using the same mixer until the dough is relatively thick. Add vinegar and lukewarm water and process until well combined.

- Using a spoon, scoop out sections and make a long baguette looking roll. You should be able to join together the different sections with your fingers.
- Place in the oven and cook for 10 minutes, then reduce the heat to 320°F and cook for another 30-40 mins. Cut and serve with olive oil and balsamic!

Nutritional Values:

Calories 197 Kcal

Total Fat 10g

Protein 14g

Dietary Fiber 3g

Carbohydrates 5g

CONCLUSION

Thank you so much for securing a copy of my book. I hope you have gotten adequate and sufficient information towards creating Keto Bread recipes.

Thanks & Stay Healthy

© Jaida Ellison

Made in the USA
Middletown, DE
19 May 2020